The New Libertarian Gospel

Pitfalls of the Theology of Liberation

The New Libertarian Gospel

Pitfalls of the Theology of Liberation

by
Father Juan Gutierrez

translated by
Paul Burns

The New Libertarian Gospel: Pitfalls of the Theology of Liberation by Father Juan Gutierrez, translated by Paul Burns from the Spanish *Teologia de la Liberacion Evaporacion de la Teologia,* Editorial Jus. Copyright © 1977 by Franciscan Herald Press, 1434 West 51st Street, Chicago, Illinois 60609.

Library of Congress Cataloging in Publication Data
Gutiérrez, Juan.
 The new libertarian gospel.

 Includes bibliographical references.
 Translation of Teología de la liberación de la teología.
 1. Gutiérrez, Gustave, 1928-   Teología de la liberación. 2. Liberation theology. I. Title.
BT83.57.G891B   261.8   77-15515
ISBN 0-8199-0682-4

NIHIL OBSTAT
 Roberto de la Rosa, M.Sp.S.
IMPRIMATUR
 Miguel Dario
 Archbishop of Mexico
 September 3, 1975

261.8

G 9851

7 901153

MADE IN THE UNITED STATES OF AMERICA

Preface

The theme of *A Theology of Liberation* is growing daily in interest and awakening more and more attention, even in circles and among people who are by nature far removed from these theological subjects.

Today, as never before, man feels himself master of technology and lord of the universe, but he also feels within himself the vacuum and the demands of matter. The world of today is one of terrifying contrasts: its suffocating materialism gives rise to a disturbing yearning for freedom of the spirit; the opulence of the powerful nations contrasts with the annihilating poverty of those that are sunk in the most deplorable conditions of life. The world of today is a huge *chiaroscuro* in which light and darkness live together in frightening symbiosis.

The problem of man today is a problem of life or death, since he no longer accepts the "outworn" idea of life after death; so sociologists, economists, philosophers, theologians, and other committed groups are seeking to find a radical solution to this terrible problem.

The "theology of liberation" has taken its place in the quest for a solution to the problems of the present day. What a shame that its partial approaches and badly used judgments and methods have distracted the honest intentions of so many who, while seeking a positive mission, have merely worsened the situation and submerged man, who is clamoring for help, even deeper in his painful and lamentable situation!

What a shame, too, that so many efforts by those who have sought to redeem man, to ennoble him and place him in his true position, have succeeded only in impoverishing him, disfiguring his genuine greatness, and tying him to an earthly horizontality, leaving him no room in which to escape from the pressures of the time and the structures of matter.

The evils of our day go beyond the limits of economics and social conditions. Man languishes and dies, not so much for lack of material food as for lack of something more deeply linked to his condition as spirit incarnate in matter. Indeed, man today feels the oppression, the suffocation, the flagellation of hunger in his body, but much more deeply he feels an anguish which oppresses his spirit to the point of paroxysm.

Under these conditions, talk of theology and liberation has become obligatory, demanding widespread attention and giving rise to careful studies. It should not surprise us that Pope Paul VI, the Second Vatican Council, and more than a few episcopal conferences have concerned themselves with this passionately interesting theme.

The theologian's task is to see man, in his special peculiarity, on his road toward God, to point out to him the courses he should follow, and to warn him of the dangers that can prevent ascension to full participation in the Divine Mystery.

This book, by Doctor Juan Gutiérrez González, analyzes the thought of one of the most distinguished exponents of this movement, which we call the theology of liberation; examines its underlying ideology, and expounds the value, extent, achievements, and limitations of his teaching. The book he examines, *A Theology of Liberation,* is the work of a namesake, Gustavo Gutiérrez. The value of the analysis lies in the fact that Dr. Gutiérrez González studies the basic aspects that this book puts forward as a solution to "this new mode of creation, analysis and solution brought by the Theology of Liberation." Its value lies, furthermore, in the fact that it analyzes each of these so-called theological insights in the light of Holy Scripture, tradition, the overall understanding of the Fathers of the Church, and the healthiest theological tradition, and thereby passes an exact judgment on the "insights" that Father Gustavo Gutiérrez proposes in his book.

Preface

It is worth pointing out that this later book does not hold back or seek refuge in ambiguous terminology for the sake of not offending susceptibilities or scandalizing readers who may be little familiar with this type of investigation. The theologian is, above all, a man who has a commitment to God and to the Church, which has entrusted him with the task of explaining, keeping, and defending the trust, and it is precisely from love for the truth that he has to be faithful and honest in his task as doctor and teacher. Paul of Tarsus knew that he had to preach the gospel, but he also knew that he had to denounce error in those who adulterated the truth.

A critical work of theology, such as this one, is a thankless task for the author. To analyze another theological work, as is done here, requires many hours of hard work and careful thought—not to mention all the research that is necessary to build a clear and certain judgment. Not for him the satisfaction of making brilliant deductions on the mystery of God or any other truth on the level of the Spirit; his is a critical work, whose spirit is continual search. The critical theologian knows that it is important to encourage every course or search in order to find new ways to the truth, but not at the cost of losing or weakening the immutable values which constitute the honor and glory of the Church.

My pleasure in being able to write these words by way of preface to this book comes not only from seeing the commitment of a genuine Latin American theologian to the liberation of man but in finding a theologian who offers a broad and full way of liberation that suits the real requirements of present-day man. This is not liberation in material things, not a magical solution to biological, economic and social needs, but liberation in the deeper sense of the word, following the action of God in history, who saves man by liberating him from eternal slavery and by crowning him with full participation in his own divine life.

RAFAEL LOPEZ, M.SP.S.

Contents

Contents

Contents

Introduction

I find myself faced with a fascinating book which has moved the spirits of many priests, religious, and lay people, particularly in Latin America. Few theological works have caused such a stir in Latin America as this one by Gustavo Gutiérrez.[1] I have read his work and meditated on it with deepest attention; now it is my task to analyze it and pronounce a theological judgment which I hope will contribute to a deepening of the science of theology, especially in South and Central America. At the outset, I make no bones about the critical bent of my study.

The work of Gustavo Gutiérrez is not lacking in merit, and this merit has shown itself in various ways in the life of the Church in Latin America. For many, indeed, it would seem that his theology has served to recall the Church and Christians to the serious and urgent tasks that face them in the struggle against social and political injustice, which still holds the greater part of mankind in conditions of life that are incompatible with human dignity.[2]

Some claim to find in this work "an effort to bring faith and life together to reconcile orthodoxy and Christian practice."[3] A typical judgment, by one who is not uncritical of other aspects of Gutiérrez's work, is this by Maximino Arias Reyero:

> It is clear that "something" is happening in Latin America and it is equally clear that something very important is happening in Latin American theology. This something is beginning now, and cannot yet be very clearly seen, but it can be seen to have a renewing force and its own determinism. The work of Gustavo Gutiérrez very clearly reflects

several positive aspects of Latin American theology. Among them, one might single out: 1. The achievement of a lay theology, that is, the insertion of the normal Christian and his real life' in the theological task; 2. A dynamic and open conception of the Church; 3. The attempt to include action as rightfully having a place in theological reflection; 4. An understanding of faith as in need of de-ideologization; 5. A serious effort to bring Christian thought up to date in dialogue with present-day secular thought; 6. The appearance of a youthful hope in a better future.

These and many other aspects make the life of theology in Latin America a pleasant and joyful one, and they also increase one's desire to work with Latin American theologians, to support their work by studying it, understanding it and spreading knowledge of it.[5]

This should show that there are theologians who see good points in the doctrinal work of Gustavo Gutiérrez. Nevertheless, despite its merits, real or supposed, it contains, in my view, serious defects that should be remedied, although I feel that some are so deeply rooted in his conception of the theology of liberation that one would be better advised to work out another theology, as we shall see in this study.

Having pointed out the critical nature of my study, it would also be well to say a word about the method I propose to follow. Let me begin with an observation that strikes me as fundamental, because it shows how difficult it is, and will continue to be, to establish a dialogue with some of those who have taken the mantle of what they insist on calling—without sufficient justification—"Latin American theology."

The trouble is that some protagonists of the theology of liberation refuse to enter into dialogue with those who do not start from or follow the same way of conceiving theology as they do. Their requirements for passing any sort of judgment on this so-called Latin American theology become so excessive that they virtually close the doors of dialogue to anyone who does not think as they do. So we reach a point where we are told that not every theologian has the right to an opinion on the theology of liberation.

What reasons are given for this? Claude Geffré, for example, in his introduction to number 96 of the review *Concilium* (1974), which is devoted to the theology of liberation, writes:

> One thing is certain: it is difficult to "convert" the theology of liberation for the sake of a would-be universal theology if one is not taking part in the struggles of those Christians actually engaged in liberating the South American continent. It is also very difficult to judge it critically from without, inasmuch as the very originality of this form of theological discourse depends on its indissolubility from real practice.[6]

One must admit that these restrictions on passing judgment on a theology, which, however original and special it may think itself, should still have God in his mystery as its *subiectum,* are surprising. How is it, then, that these same theologians have been able to pass judgment on "European theology," which they find so alien to themselves?

Geffré's claim is even more strange when we find that this "Latin American theology" has frequent recourse to Dutch, English, French, German, Spanish, and other Europeans in the sources and authorities it falls back on. I am happy to "belong" to the Latin American continent, but I have to ask myself if I fulfill the requirement of "participating in the struggles of committed Christians in the process of liberation of the continent of South America," for Geffré continues:

> The theologian who is worthy of the name cannot now be merely a student of scripture and the tradition of the Church. He has to be defined by the most rigorous understanding of the process of liberation as it has come about in the Latin American continent and, naturally, such knowledge will come to be inseparable from effective par-

ticipation in revolutionary struggles for the liberation of
the poor.[7]

There is surely a legitimate objection to be made to these
requirements that would condition the right of a theologian to
judge a theology, because they are precisely what has to be
proved. Where indeed, and with what validity, have these
"theologians of praxis" proved that it is only in and from praxis,
as they understand the term, that it is possible to interpret the
word of God? Furthermore, what sort of "effective participation
in the revolutionary struggles for the liberation of the poor" is
one talking about when we are told that such knowledge is
inseparable from the work of any theologian who is worthy of
the name? Again, is it not true that theology deals with the very
mysteries that we *hold* to be true, whose truth and meaning
theology seeks to penetrate? Theology is not applied to the
phenomenon of faith but to the *truths* of faith that faith itself
tries to assimilate.

Yet such points carry no weight with Geffré, who goes on to
say:

> There is a displacement of the central concern of theology,
> which is no longer exclusively the *intellectus fidei,* but an
> understanding of action in the name of Christ: that is, the
> perception of the forms that love should assume in a spe-
> cific situation. . . . [8]
> Because there can be no hiatus between faith and social
> practice, it is practice which will judge the truth of a
> theology. . . . [The contributors to this issue] base their
> answer [to the risk involved in this approach] on a theolo-
> gy of the Holy Spirit.[9]

Here we touch on the basic problem, which has to be studied
and cannot be taken as already established. The real question is
this: Does the theological concept of truth intrinsically include
its particular historical efficacy?[10]

The problems posed by such an extreme approach as that of

Geffré, who seeks thereby to preclude any judgments on the theology of liberation that come from "outside" it, gave me the idea of criticizing Gustavo Gutiérrez's book from "within." This, then, is the basis of my critical approach to Gutiérrez's book and the method by which I hope to study it.

There can and must be a theology of salvation and genuine liberation. What I am criticizing here is not so much a theology of liberation but its presentation in the work of Gustavo Gutiérrez. If one is looking for a true attempt at establishing an authentic theology of liberation, one should turn, it seems to me, to a recent work by Yves Congar.[11]

Chapter 1
The "Theology of Liberation" as Seen from Within

Following the method set out in the introduction, I propose to devote this first chapter to a presentation of the thought of Gustavo Gutiérrez. We will not, at first, make any judgments or pose any questions but merely set out his thought in a straightforward manner, leaving appreciations, questions, praise, and criticism to a later stage.

The first chapter of his book, *A Theology of Liberation,* is the basic one, since, as Geffré says, "It implies a commotion in theology." His later chapters are affected by the new view of theological discourse that he sets out in the first chapter.

The Classic Tasks of Theology and Theology as Critical Reflection on Praxis

"Theological reflection—that is, the understanding of the faith—arises spontaneously and inevitably in the believer, in all those who have accepted the gift of the Word of God."[1] These opening lines serve principally to establish the link between theology and the life of faith that seeks to be authentic and complete and is therefore essential to the ecclesial community. It is on this foundation that the edifice of theology, in the technical and precise sense of the term, can be built. This foundation is not only the starting point but the soil, as it were, in which theological reflection grows.[2]

Quoting Duquoc and Congar and with reference to Comblin,[3] Gutiérrez states that there has been a change in the way theolo-

1

gy is understood.[4] This observation introduces the theme of "the classic tasks of theology." He alludes to the fact that theology has been dependent upon the historical development of the Church and that it has exercised different functions throughout history.[5] But "this does not necessarily mean that any of these different approaches has today been definitively superseded. Although expressed in different ways, the essential effort to understand the faith has remained."[6] From this he logically concludes that, despite historical conditioning, there are permanent tasks for theology; the classic ones can be considered as theology as wisdom and theology as rational knowledge.[7]

Theology as Wisdom

Gutiérrez's next section deals with the permanent function of theology as wisdom, from the early centuries of the Church to the fourteenth century, and in a sense down to our times. He says that theology was closely linked to the spiritual life and was essentially meditation on the Bible, geared toward spiritual growth. It was above all monastic and therefore "characterized by a spiritual life removed from worldly concerns."[8] Anxious to conduct dialogue with the thought of its time, this theology used Platonic and neo-Platonic categories.[9] In these categories it found a metaphysics more attentive to the absolute than to life on this earth. In the fourteenth century, a rift appeared between theology and spirituality, and we are still suffering, to a certain extent, from the consequences of this in our time. Finally, he stresses that this function of theology is permanent.

Theology as Rational Knowledge

From the twelfth century on, theology began to establish itself as a science: "The transition has been made from *sacra pagina* to *theologia* in the modern sense which Abelard . . . was the first to use."[10] This process culminated with Albert the Great and Thomas Aquinas on the basis of Aristotelian categories. Theology was classified as a "subaltern science."[11] For St. Thomas, however, "theology is not only a science but also wisdom flowing from the charity which unites man to God."[12]

Turning to the notion of science that is applicable to theology, Gutiérrez tells us that the Thomistic idea of science is unclear today, since it does not correspond to the definition that is generally acceptable to the modern mind. We have to remember, he tells us, quoting Dumont, that "the essential feature of St. Thomas Aquinas' work is that theology is an intellectual discipline born of the meeting of faith and reason."[13] So it would seem that it is more accurate to regard the theological task as rational knowledge rather than as science.

This also is a permanent function of theology, since it deals with the meeting between faith and reason—not exclusively between faith and any one philosophy or even between faith and philosophy in general. Today, there are many manifestations of reason other than philosophical ones, and the understanding of faith can be found in the social, psychological, and biological sciences.[14] After the thirteenth century, he tells us, "there is a degradation of the thomistic concept of theology . . . the demands of rational knowledge will be reduced to the need for systematization and clear exposition. Scholastic theology will gradually become . . . an ancillary discipline of the magisterium of the Church, its function will be: (1) to define, present and explain revealed truths; (2) to examine doctrine, to denounce and condemn false doctrines and to defend true ones; (3) to teach revealed truths authoritatively."[15]

After his analysis of what he takes to be St. Thomas' understanding of the scientific function of theology, which should perhaps better be described as rational knowledge than as a science, Gutiérrez sums up by stating that both the wisdom and the science aspects of theology are permanent and indispensable functions of all theological thinking. "However, both functions must be salvaged at least partially from the division and deformations they have suffered throughout history. A reflective outlook and style especially must be retained rather than one or another specific achievement gained in a historical context different from ours."[16]

Theology as Critical Reflection on Praxis

This is a function of theology which has gradually become more clearly defined in recent years but which has antecedents in the early centuries of the Church. St. Augustine in his *City of God*, for example, shows a capacity for true analysis of the signs of the times and "the demands with which they challenge the Christian community." Gutiérrez's study of this concept of theology as critical reflection on praxis is divided into two subsections. The first is titled "Historical Praxis" and the second "Critical Reflection."

"Historical Praxis"

In this section the author of *A Theory of Liberation* tries to show the different factors which stress, particularly in our days, the existential and active aspects of Christian life. These factors he defines as the following, basing himself on the authority and on his study of different authors (the means by which he has recourse to these authors is something we shall deal with later):

(a) The rediscovery of charity as the center of the Christian life.

(b) A more biblical view of the act of faith—that is, faith as a commitment to God and neighbor, a total response of man to God, who saves through love—so that "the understanding of the faith appears as the understanding not of the simple affirmation—almost memorization—of truths, but of a commitment, an overall attitude, a particular posture toward life."[17]

(c) The evolution of Christian spirituality—a process that culminates today in studies on the religious value of the profane and the spirituality of the activity of the Christian in the world.

(d) Sensitivity to the anthropological aspects of revelation. The consequence of this is a revaluation of the presence and activity of man in the world, particularly in relation to other men. There is no "horizontalism" in this but simply the rediscovery of the indissoluble unity of man and God.

(e) The very life of the Church appears ever more clearly as a *locus theologicus.*

(f) The word of God "gathers and is incarnated in the community of faith which gives itself to the service of all men."

(g) A theology of the signs of the times. These signs are not only to call to intellectual analysis but above all to pastoral activity, to commitment, and to service. So, as the Vatican Council pointed out,[18] the particular function of theologians will be to contribute to a greater clarity about this commitment by means of intellectual analysis.

(h) A factor of a philosophical nature "reinforces the importance of human action as the point of departure for all reflection."

(i) The influence of Marxist thought. This focuses on praxis and is geared to the transformation of the world: "Marxism as the formal framework of temporary philosophical thought cannot be superseded."[19] Be this as it may, it is a fact that contemporary theology finds itself in direct and fruitful confrontation with Marxism. It is largely due to the stimulus of Marxism that theological thought has begun to reflect on the meaning of the transformation of this world and the action of man in history. Thanks to this confrontation, theology can perceive what its efforts at understanding the faith receive from the historical praxis of man in history, as well as what its own reflection might mean for the transformation of the world.[20]

(j) Finally, there is the rediscovery of the eschatological dimension in theology, which leads to a consideration of the central role of historical praxis. If history is an opening to the future, then history is a task, a political occupation. It is man's task to build history, and man thereby opens himself to the gift which gives history transcendent meaning: the full and definitive encounter with the Lord and with other men. Faith in God is not only not foreign to the transformation of the world but leads necessarily to the building of brotherhood and communion in history. The aim here is not to deny the meaning of orthodoxy but "to balance and even to reject the primacy and almost exclusiveness which doctrine has enjoyed in Christian life" and, in a more positive vein, to recognize the importance of deeds, action, and praxis in the Christian life.

"Critical Reflection"

These factors lead us to a more accurate understanding, on the one hand, of the meaning of communion with the Lord and, on the other, the need to produce an explicit formulation of the function of theology as critical reflection.[21] Gutiérrez then defines his understanding of theology as critical reflection and he distinguishes three levels on which theology is critical thought:

(a) Man's critical reflection on himself, on his own basic principles. This is required if theology is to act in full possession of its conceptual elements.

(b) It also has to take a clear critical attitude toward economic and sociocultural issues in the life and reflection of the Christian community.

(c) It also has to be a criticism of society and the Church, "insofar as they are called and addressed by the Word of God; . . . a critical theory worked out in the light of the Word, accepted in faith and inspired by a practical purpose—and therefore indissolubly linked to historical praxis."

It is this third level of "critical reflection" that Gutiérrez sees as the most important. The Christian community has to profess "a faith which works through charity," and this has to be real charity—action and commitment to the service of men. Theology has to come after this: "Theology is reflection, a critical attitude. Theology *follows;* it is the second step." The pastoral activity of the Church "does not flow as a conclusion from theological premises. Theology does not produce pastoral activity; rather it reflects upon it." The life of the Church and its historical commitment become "a privileged *locus theologicus* for understanding the faith."[22]

Reflecting on the presence and action of the Christian in the world means being open to the world and gathering the questions it poses—a point of critical importance. Reflection in the light of faith as a constant accompaniment to the pastoral action of the Church safeguards society and the Church from regarding as permanent what is only temporary. This will constitute the difference between theology and ideologies that rationalize and justify particular social and ecclesial orders. "On the other hand, theology, by pointing to the sources of revelation helps to orient pastoral activity; it puts it in a wider context and so helps to avoid activism and immediatism."[23]

As "critical reflection" on society and the Church, theology is an understanding that grows and is in a way changeable, since the commitment of the Christian community takes different forms throughout history. The understanding of this commitment also has to be constantly renewed and will sometimes take untrodden paths. Gutiérrez quotes Bouillard's phrase: "A theology which is not up-to-date is a false theology."[24] Insofar as theology interprets historical events with the intention of revealing and proclaiming their profound meaning, it performs a prophetic function. This reading of events has the purpose of making the Christian's commitment within them clearer and more radical. So, in the final analysis, the "true" interpretation of the meaning revealed by theology will be found in specific times and places; we have here "a political hermeneutics of the Gospel."[25]

Gutiérrez's Conclusion to Chapter 1

Gutiérrez's conclusion to his first chapter shows us how the "critical" function of theology—as he describes it—relates to what he has called "the classic tasks of theology": theology as wisdom and theology as rational knowledge. This will give rise, he trusts, to a kind of theology that "will perhaps give us the solid and permanent, albeit modest foundation for the theology in a Latin-American perspective which is both desired and needed." Furthermore, if, as Harvey Cox has said, "the only future that theology has, one might say, is to become the theology of the future,"[26] this means that the "theology of the future" has to be what will assure the future of theology, which in turn means that it must necessarily be critical reflection on historical praxis in the way he has sketched: "to reflect on a forward-directed action is not to concentrate on the past . . . rather it is to penetrate the present reality, the movement of history, that which is driving history toward the future."[27] It is to reflect in the light of a future which is believed in and hoped for, and to reflect with a view to action which transforms the present. This means "sinking roots where the pulse of history is beating at this moment"—and not from an armchair.

This, then, is Gustavo Gutiérrez's thought as set out in his basic chapter. It would be difficult to summarize it further since each paragraph contains an important idea and has to be taken into account.

Chapter 2
A Criticism of Gutiérrez's Chapter 1 from Within

In order to make a valid objective judgment on Gustavo Gutiérrez's thought, from which I differ on several basic points, I propose to examine his chapter from within, so to speak, and to analyze it in its various elements, as he presents them. As a start, I would like to take the following points:

1. The authorities he quotes in his work
2. The classic functions of theology
3. The factors that have led to his conception of theology as critical reflection on praxis
4. The critical function of theology

The Authorities Quoted in the Book of Gustavo Gutiérrez

A glance at the notes to his first chapter produces an impression of a vast array of quoted authors and works. There is a long list of names of the great European and a lesser number of Latin American theologians: Congar, Chenu, Rahner, Kasper, Bouyer, de Lubac, Duquoc, Thils, von Baltasar, Häring, Spicq, Alfaro, Schillebeeckx, Ratzinger, Dumont, Metz, Moltmann, Comblin, Jossua, Liégé, Cottier, and others of scarcely less importance.[1]

This is an impressive array, but in some ways the impression it makes is strange. This is supposed to be a "Latin American" theology, but except for Pironio, Sánchez Vázquez, and Mariategui, the authors he quotes are all European. His main theme and preoccupation is the problems that face "the most committed Christian groups"[2] in Latin America and their activities, but one can ask whether his constant recourse to European thinkers does not detract from the originality he claims.[3]

However, a more important factor overrides the straitjacket in which he would place any theologian who tries to judge this particular theology for which such claims of originality are made. A theology is distinguished more by the viewpoint from which it studies theological themes than by the themes or problems it concerns itself with. So even if we concede that the problems of Latin America are in many cases different from those in Europe, this is not enough to make an original theology. When one considers the problems of Latin America in the same light as illuminates European theology, the theology of Latin America does not appear all that original. So, again, one can study Latin American problems, but doing so with the support of European authorities is not enough to give this work the originality that has been claimed for it.

I have said that I was struck by the number of references Gutiérrez makes in the relatively few pages of his first chapter to nearly all the outstanding theologians of the present day. This fact alone makes it worth examining the critical apparatus used by the author, and I must admit that I have taken the trouble to read all the sources that Gutiérrez quotes; this has been a long process, but it seems to me to be fruitful. It was also necessary, if I was to justify my claim to criticize this work "from within."

In his excellent study on St. Thomas Aquinas, Chenu studies the process of documentation employed by St. Thomas.[4] "If one is trying to study a modern author," Chenu says, "it would be of little interest to examine the way in which he collected his documentation—except for the most narrow academic interest." (He then gives reasons why he considers St. Thomas a different case.) But when I came to the work of Gustavo Gutiérrez I had further reasons (perhaps they might be called malice or at least suspicion) for adopting this process. My purpose was to find out whether all these prominent theologians in fact uphold the conclusions that Gutiérrez draws from them.

So let us turn to the critical apparatus. Its faults are not principally errors;[5] there is something more serious than this: inexactitude, lack of fidelity in transmitting the thought of the authors he quotes, and distortion of their thoughts in the way he uses them.

Inexactitudes

These vary in importance. It does not matter very much if an author is quoted inexactly when one is dealing with something that is generally accepted. It *does* matter, on the other hand, when the authority is quoted in order to supply a premise from which a conclusion can be drawn, particularly if this conclusion is to appear to be of startling originality. I find examples of both types of imprecision in this work.

Gutiérrez makes his statements, which I shall turn to later, and to support or confirm them he refers to other authors in such a general manner that there is no way of telling whether they really support what he thinks.[6] See, for example, his note 9: "The works of Guardini, Congar, Voillaume, Evely, Paoli, Régamey and many others are examples of this effort," or note 12, which is supposed to support an interesting statement that "on the basis of Aristotelian categories, theology was classified as a subaltern science." The note reads: "*Summa Theologica,* I, Q. 1; see also Congar, 'Théologie', *Foi et Théologie,* and *Situations et tâches;* Comblin, *Teología católica;* and M. D. Chenu, OP, 'Is Theology a Science?' trans. A. H. N. Green Armytage (New York, Hawthorn Books, 1959)."[7]

Is this really a serious methodology, and how can one enter into a meaningful discussion with an author who makes so many points of view his own?

But there is something more serious and significant, his use of "partial" quotes. There are many places where he quotes eminent theologians but takes only one part of the text and omits the other part, which would balance the part he quotes. He does this even when the balancing part is only a few lines away in the article or book he is alluding to. There are other occasions, and this strikes me as even more serious, when the author he adduces as an authority tends to think rather the opposite of what Gutiérrez uses him to show. This sort of assertion obviously needs support; so let us examine the critical method he uses.

Partial Quotes

One of the factors that Gutiérrez claims justifies the critical function of theology, as he understands it, is the presence and activity of man in the world, particularly in relation to other men. In support of this he quotes the following text from Congar:

> Seen as a whole, the direction of theological thinking has been characterized by a transference away from attention to the being *per se* of supernatural realities and toward attention to their relationship with man, with the world and with the problems and the affirmations of all those who for us represent the *Others*.[8]

This text can be seen to bear some relation to what Gutiérrez says a little further on, although it is not the same thing:

> The goal is to balance and even to reject the primacy and almost exclusiveness which doctrine has enjoyed in Christian life and above all to modify the emphasis, often obsessive, upon the attainment of an orthodoxy which is often nothing more than fidelity to obsolete tradition or a debatable interpretation. In a more positive vein the intention is to recognise the work and importance of concrete behaviour, of deeds, of action, of praxis in the Christian life.[9]

I would like to ask why Gutiérrez does not continue his quote from Congar, since this is what immediately follows:

> It is not that theologians turned from the contemplation
> of God and his mysteries to a pure earthly humanism: this
> would be a betrayal and they have not committed it. The
> scrutinizing of mysteries in themselves is never a waste of
> time and sometimes what is most unactual can soon bear
> considerable fruit in the most earthly actuality.[10]

Four pages further on, he quotes Congar again,[11] and again I am struck by the partiality of this quote. Could this be because he is interested in only one aspect of what Congar says, both here and in the earlier quote, and in his references to Chenu? The part of their text that stresses the necessity of the "Facts of Revelation" for theology is not mentioned. Why not?

The same thing happens with his references to Chenu.[12] The text he quotes[13] deserves a double comment: on the one hand, according to Gutiérrez, it refers to "the participation of Christians in the important social movements of their time"; on the other hand, according to Chenu himself, this text refers to something broader than mere social participation, which is mentioned only in fifth place.[14] The second and more important point is that Gutiérrez omits any mention of the "Facts of Revelation" which Chenu refers to in the same article, where he says:

> Theological "reason" can have no success nor can it
> operate except in the area where and to the extent that it
> has entered—or rather incessantly penetrated—in the
> light of faith, into religious possession of the Facts of
> Revelation of the "Word of God." Only if it follows this
> strict and total coherence can a theology be built up.[15]

This text is only a few pages before that quoted by Gutiérrez. A little further on, just one page after the text he quotes, Chenu stresses the point again:

> This is therefore the law of theological understanding
> and consequently the reason for the cycle of positive disci-

plines that binds one to its service: the Facts of Revelation have preference, not only the dialectical primacy of an edict but a *presence* with the inexhaustible realism and silent insistence implied by the word to those who have accepted it. On this basis one can now "build."[16]

Quotations Used in the Opposite Sense

Following his tendency to eliminate or at least diminish the doctrinal aspect of faith and of theology, Gutiérrez tells us that

> according to the Bible, faith is the total response of man to God, who saves through love. In this light the understanding of the faith appears as the understanding not of the simple affirmation—almost memorization—of truths, but of a commitment, an overall attitude, a particular posture toward life[17]

What sources does Gustavo Gutiérrez quote in support of this viewpoint?

Leaving a deeper examination of what the act of faith actually implies and its repercussions on the theological task for later, let us for the moment concentrate on two of the authors referred to on the subject that Gutiérrez has just proposed to us; these authors are Alfaro and Spicq.[18] Is it really true that in the article by Alfaro, which he quotes, the understanding of faith is seen as "the understanding . . . of a commitment, an overall attitude, a particular posture toward life"? It is a pity that Gutiérrez has not made his thought clearer on this point—as indeed happened with his quotes from Congar and Chenu. Does he really mean the disjunctive: "understanding not of the simple affirmation . . . but of a commitment"? Would it not have been clearer to say: "understanding not only of simple affirmation . . . but also of a commitment"? This could be either an oversight or an example of the tendency we have already noted: to diminish the importance of doctrine both in revelation and in theology. This is an important point, since it seems to me that we are dealing with a deliberate intention rather than a mere slip.

If we examine the Alfaro article referred to, we will find that Gutiérrez does not quote a particular page but just the pages in the review in which it appears, which is taken up by the whole article (pp. 463–505). I think it worthwhile to quote in full the closing paragraphs of Alfaro's article, which are a synthesis of the analysis he made throughout the forty pages of the article:

> Johannine faith can be said to show the following particular characteristics: (a) the principality of the aspect of knowledge which is more intense in John than in Paul himself; (b) the mission and the divine sonship of Jesus are set out as the main object of faith; (c) Christ is at once he in whom one believes and he whom one believes. The faith of men knows God through the means of Christ, who sees and reveals the Father; (d) belief exists in a close connection with the witness of Christ and of God through Christ; (e) belief enables man to possess eternal life here and now.[19]

> There is a striking resemblance between John and Paul's concept (and even terminology) of faith and of its importance for man's salvation: through faith man becomes a participant in the saving event of Christ and receives eternal life: faith includes adherence of the whole man to Christ and communion of life with Him, Himself and through Him with God. Johannine faith, just like Pauline and what has been described in the Acts of the Apostles, is Christocentric.

> An analysis of the whole biblical terminology shows that the concept of faith is basically identical in both the Old and the New Testaments: belief includes the total adherence of man to God, who reveals himself by saving. Within this total relationship of man various elements are contained and their importance and visibility differs between the Old and the New Testaments. The aspect of man's obedience to God is constant and immutable in the whole biblical description of faith. But while the faith of the Old Testament expresses confidence in the divine promises as a primary element and is less explicit on the element of understanding of God's interventions than on

the aspect of trust in God, *the faith of the New Testament lays primary stress on the aspect of understanding and makes the element of trust in God less visible.*[20]

However, we are not dealing with a divergence in the concept of faith itself, but rather with a different stress given to one or another element in the same concept. The faith of the Old and the New Testaments are not different realities, there is just a certain shift of stress or coloration, but they both refer to one and the same reality.

The principal reason for this shift lies in the event that divides the Old from the New Testament: the event of Christ. The aspect of understanding in faith becomes primary because faith has been changed into an acceptance of the apostolic preaching concerning the Christ event. The first appearance of this phenomenon is found in the Acts: *believing* then comes to mean acceptance of the Christian kerygma as true (cf. Acts 2:44; 4:4, 32; 8:13; 11:21). In the Synoptics one can see that the shift of accent from the acceptance of trust to that of understanding occurs when faith is referred to concerning Jesus as the Christ (Mk 15:32; Mt 27:42; Lk 23:35; etc.) or concerning his Resurrection (Mk 16:11, 13, 14). The work of Paul and John is in its totality orientated to the saving mystery of the Death-Resurrection of Christ or his mission—divine sonship—and *in them the element of understanding becomes pre-eminent.*[21]

In chapter eleven of the Letter to the Hebrews the aspect of trust becomes the principal in faith once again, since this whole chapter describes the faith of the men of the Old Testament. All this shows that the pre-eminence given to the aspect of understanding in New Testament faith coincides with its Christocentric approach: the event of Christ, the definitive saving intervention of God promised in the Old Testament. Man's response to God in faith includes acceptance of this divine intervention as true in the first place; therefore the aspect of understanding is primary in New Testament faith, but since the event of Christ has a basically eschatological meaning and looks to the second coming of Christ and the saving consummation

of humanity, the faith of the New Testament includes
trust and the expectation of the future salvation that will
be brought about through Christ and with Christ.[22]

We find the same phenomenon at work when Gutiérrez
vaguely refers to Spicq. He might at least have looked at the
analytical index in Spicq's book, which would have been enough
to show him that this biblical scholar sees faith as essentially an
understanding. At no moment does he deny the aspect of adherence to the person of Christ in the form of trust, but what is not
permissible is a devaluing of the doctrinal content of faith and
of adherence to truth, such as Gutiérrez presents us with.

Thus there is sometimes a large gap between the conclusions
drawn by Gutiérrez and the authorities he quotes as favoring his
opinion. His critical apparatus shows the defects we have mentioned. I believe there is something more than distraction, print-
ing errors, or haste in this. This something-rather-more, on the
other hand, seems to prepare the ground for the "new way to
do theology" that the author of *A Theology of Liberation* offers
us.

Having established this, we can set the critical apparatus aside
and pass directly to a study of the subject matter of the different
parts of Gutiérrez's first chapter.

Chapter 3
The Classic Functions of Theology

In this chapter I propose to examine Gutiérrez's account of what he sees as the two classical functions of theology and its permanent tasks: theology as wisdom and theology as rational knowledge. In the two succeeding chapters I will examine his concept of theology as critical reflection.

Theology as Wisdom

I have already outlined Gutiérrez's account of the historical development of theology in the first centuries of the Church; so I will not repeat it here. He tries to tell us what theology was about in the early centuries of the Church; however, his account does not mention any century, except the fourteenth. Is it really sufficient, to give us an idea of what happened in these fourteen centuries, simply to say, as he does, that theology was "meditation on the Bible geared toward spiritual growth"? And particularly as he adds that it was a monastic theology and was therefore "characterized by a spiritual life removed from worldly concerns"? His final comment is that the use of Platonic and neo-Platonic categories led to the present life's not being valued sufficiently, although he stresses that the Greek fathers went well beyond mere personal spiritual meditation and placed theology in a wider and more fruitful context.[1]

Given that this function of theology appears in such a poor light—"above all monastic," failing to value the present life sufficiently, and "removed from worldly concerns"—we might ask why it continues to be so important; in other words, what is the permanent element in it that should be retained? Gutiérrez says something on this point later, when he speaks of theology as critical reflection on praxis in the light of faith. My feeling is that he would not like to see much of it left, but he had to mention it to display his erudition (although he devotes only a page to it), and that he undervalues this particular classic function of theology, theology as wisdom.

I think, however, that one has to go further and ask whether his vision of theology as wisdom is not altogether too simplistic. Has he, for example, really given an account of the theology of St. Augustine by including it in "a meditation on the Bible geared toward spiritual growth"?[2] Or take, for example, the thought of St. Irenaeus as described by Congar: "a theology entirely within the ambit of faith, interpreting the faith, the whole relevant to the preservation of the truth of the saving religious event based on Christ." And again: "without working out a systematic theology he is concerned to think of faith as a coherent unity and of the redeeming work of the Incarnate Word as inserted in a broad vision of the history of man and the world."[3] In the same work, speaking of the theological thought of the fathers in general (excluding St. Augustine, whom he considers elsewhere), he says: "The general tenor of the act of theology in the Fathers is such that the activity of thinking is separated neither from the life nor from the pastoral necessities of the Church . . . nor from the spiritual life and the framework of monastic or clerical life as liturgical and ascetic life."[4]

Is it true, furthermore, to say that this theology of the first centuries was above all monastic? Evidently not.[5] Nor is it true to say that the monastic theologians were abstracted from the world to such an extent that they were incapable of entering into dialogue with it. Those pastors mentioned by Hans Urs Von Baltasan, who were frequently doctors, and who may or may not have been monks or connected with the monastic life, can hardly be said to have practiced a theology "characterized by a spiritual life removed from worldly concern."[6]

This vision of the history of theology is really too simplistic.

If Gutiérrez wishes to conclude that theology has to be more deeply inserted in the world if it is to live in the logic of faith, there is no need for him to employ such a distorted presentation of the history of theology. If it is really as he says, why is it so important and why should this wisdom aspect of theology be permanent? There is no need of theology for a meditation on the Bible that is geared toward spiritual growth. If he sees it as monastic and removed from worldly concerns or as failing to value the present life sufficiently because it depended on neo-Platonic categories, I cannot see that his conclusion that this spiritual function constitutes a permanent dimension of theology can be sustained.

Theology as Rational Knowledge

In his next section Gutiérrez shows us something of the originality of St. Thomas Aquinas in the history of theology: to see theology as "not only a science but also wisdom."[7] Before examining what Gutiérrez considers essential in the scientific aspect of theology, let us see what he tells us about this aspect according to St. Thomas Aquinas; then let us see if his interpretation actually coincides with that of the Angelic Doctor.

He tells us that, for St. Thomas, theology is not only a science but also wisdom. Is this justifiable? In an attempt to interpret St. Thomas' thought, Gutiérrez links wisdom to the charity "which unites man to God." So wisdom—supposing we are talking of theology as wisdom—flows from charity. Is this really St. Thomas' thought as expressed in the first question of the *Summa Theologica?*

St. Thomas speaks of "Holy Doctrine" as wisdom in article 6 of the first question of the *Summa.* His doctrine in this article can be summed up in the following affirmations.

Theology—"Holy Doctrine"—is truly wisdom and preeminent wisdom. Wisdom differs from science in that wisdom consists of a knowledge of realities, not only through knowledge of their lower causes but also through knowledge of their higher

causes. The task of theology, as such, is to examine the highest
cause of the entire universe, God himself. Furthermore, theology is wisdom in the highest degree because it not only considers
God to the extent that it reaches him through conclusions that
stem from knowledge of creatures, as is the case with natural
theology, but, in the case of Christian theology, on the other
hand, considers God according to his own inner life and takes
not creatures but God himself as the principle of this knowledge.
In this way it becomes wisdom to the highest degree, or knowldege through the highest causes, or the supreme reasons behind
things. As wisdom, it orders and judges everything, including its
own principles, by defending them and explaining them. In this
sense it is like a measure and a rule that perfects all the other
sciences.

What St. Thomas says in his reply to the third objection[8] is
very important, and it is precisely this that Gutiérrez appears
to leave out of account. While he claims that for St. Thomas
theology is a science as such, in direct relation with charity, for
St. Thomas it is a science insofar as it is knowledge of the things
of God. It is knowledge acquired through study, although it
always takes its principles from revelation (ad 3). The reply St.
Thomas gives refers to the distinction—not to say the total lack
of relationship—between strictly theological knowledge and the
knowledge of the mystics.[9] These are two distinct ways of knowing God, who has revealed himself to us and whom we have
received through faith.

Does this mean that there can be no close relationship between the rational discursive knowledge of theology and mystical contemplation? By no means; the contrary is true. The
Christian can develop his faith on two levels, that of knowledge
through concepts and reasoned reflection and that of knowledge
from experience and the direct influence of the Holy Spirit.
Furthermore, there is a natural intercommunion between the
two forms of knowledge in the mind of the theologian who is
impelled toward mystical theology through notional theology.
If he is not impelled in this way, if he does not feel the lack that

notional theology leaves in his believer's spirit, he will be deficient as a theologian, however exact his science.

Gutiérrez does not explain what St. Thomas understands by theology as wisdom—that it is closely related to what Thomas understands as knowledge of the gifts of the Holy Spirit.[10]

But theology is also a science. Gutiérrez considers "the essential feature of St. Thomas Aquinas's work is that theology is an intellectual discipline born of the meeting of faith and reason."[11] At this point we must consider what Gutiérrez tells us of theology as rational knowledge, because this is where he gently, almost imperceptibly, inserts his "new way of doing theology." The essential element of Thomas Aquinas' great work has to be retained. But what is the essential element? It would appear to be only that theology is an intellectual discipline born of the meeting between faith and reason. But reason, Gutiérrez says, does not mean any one philosophy, or even philosophy in general. Today, reason has many other manifestations: "the social, psychological and biological sciences." In Latin America, he continues, the social sciences (for example) are extremely important. The Scholastic attempt to rationalize theology after St. Thomas involved a "degradation of the thomastic concept of theology."[12] After the Council of Trent, it became an ancillary discipline of the magisterium of the Church, with set functions, which were "(1) to define, present and explain revealed truths; (2) to examine doctrine, to denounce and condemn false doctrines, and to defend true ones; (3) to teach revealed truths authoritatively."

This is *not* what is essential in the theology of St. Thomas, which is the meeting between faith and reason. Now, reason can be manifested in sociology; in other words, according to Gutiérrez, theology can be a meeting between faith and sociology. Just one more step is needed, which is that, in the meeting between faith and sociology, sociology can determine the content of faith, as we shall see.

Would St. Thomas see himself faithfully interpreted in this? I do not think so. It is true that Gutiérrez is not talking about the Thomas Aquinas of the thirteenth century in Europe but about Thomas Aquinas as applicable today in Latin America. So he claims that the accidental elements in Thomas' thought can be sacrificed without sacrificing the essential: the simple meeting between faith and reason—or reason sufficiently and opportunely represented by the social, biological, or psychological sciences. Does this retain the essential of theology as a science, as St. Thomas saw it? Again, I cannot believe it does.

Let us turn now to the Angelic Doctor himself and see the essential elements of his concept of theological reasoning.[13]

First, where does theology spring from? It is true, and Gutiérrez notes it, that theology springs from the meeting between faith and human intelligence. It is a vital reaction of human intelligence, which reasons on the truths it knows from revelation and to which it adheres through faith. Theology springs from the activation of faith in an intelligence that is avid to understand and is subject to the law of progress. In the innermost spirit is a confrontation between faith, which is pure submission to the understanding of the word of God, and reasoning, which is, on the contrary, a quest for explanations and therefore a questioning of the intelligible aspects of the object.[14]

Therefore, if it is true that theology is the fruit of the meeting between faith and human reason, it does not spring from a casual encounter between them. The theological proceeding is made necessary because faith is what it is and because reason is what it is. Faith does not render the proceedings of reason useless. Revealed truths are received by human intelligence, and these truths transmit something that is intelligible to human intelligence. Human intelligence can reach this intelligibility through faith and can pronounce a judgment on these truths. There is in this something more than the objective presentation of truths; there is also an intrinsic elevation of human understanding which, by placing it on the level of what can be understood about God, allows it to reach, by means of and through signs, the mysterious, signified reality. Human understanding is thereby elevated precisely as a principle of the reasoning process. Therefore the faith of theology, instead of paralyzing the reasoning faculty, stimulates it and opens it to new topics of understanding, without in any way modifying the conditions under which this faculty has to be exercised by reason of its union with the body.[15]

The revelation of truth and of the divine reality, which is simple and whole, is adapted to the human role of understanding. Revelation then multiplies this one truth and reality in a plurality of particular truths which, by reason of their inner order, reproduce in their own way the original unity from which they sprang; they lead man's mind to this unity. By conforming to rational human intelligence, these truths are themselves rational: one depends on the other intrinsically; some explain others. Revelation guarantees only each truth that it proposes, and *believing* consists in adhering to each and every one, not because of the validity of the explanation but because they are based on the authority of God, who reveals them.

But these truths, in which man believes, carry their explanatory truth within themselves. This is when the understanding of the believer is obliged, through its own dynamism, to *organize* these truths according to their inner order.[16] The deep intention of this organizing process is to come to an understanding, not of a new truth but of what has been revealed and what the believer has accepted through faith in a more complete manner. There is no way of coming to an understanding of the faith except through reason, since the understanding that comes into contact with faith is not *any* understanding but an understanding that reasons.[17] One might say that the light of faith espouses the light of human intelligence, directs it, and uses it to form its object in a body of doctrine in a rational and scientific manner.[18] One might also say that the scientific nature of theology springs not from any encounter between faith and human understanding but from that which emanates from a sort of incarnation of the truth in the very essence of our spirit.

"Theology," says Chenu, "is of a piece with the theandric mystery of the Word of God, the Word made flesh." The entry of truth in the believing reason will have, as a result, "the mobilization of the techniques of reason within and for the mystic perception of the believer: conceptual division, multiplication of analyses and judgments, definitions and divisions, comparisons and classifications, inferences, inquiries in search of explanation and . . . deduction, since the characteristic operation of science is deduction, which is where the process of rationalization reaches its true efficacy."[19] This process of deduction should be understood not only as a way of reaching new truths but of reaching a new, basic understanding of the intelligibility of another truth.

In this way one can see how theology is born and how, for St. Thomas, it became a scientific discipline. Since the theologian, according to the workings of his intelligence-reason, seeks a better understanding of faith from within faith itself, he *organizes,* he looks for unity, coherence, and order; to arrive at a better understanding, he operates scientifically. Faith unfolds and develops in reason's obeying the laws of a human wisdom. Among these laws, those that are particularly appropriate to theology are a requirement for order (II, II, 8–1, ab ad 1) and a requirement of unity in the objects of knowledge.[20] The principal work of theology as a rational science will consist in the construction of what has been revealed. Analogy (cf. I, q. 1, a 5 ad 2) will play a very important part in this construction, as will the connection between one mystery and another.

A word, now, about the theory of subaltern sciences which permitted St. Thomas to make a definitive assessment of the scientific status of theology. When Aquinas speaks of the subalternation of theological science, he says that this proceeds from "principles known through the light of another superior science, which is the science of God and of the blessed" (I, q. Ia, 2). It is interesting to examine why he speaks of the "science of God and of the blessed."[21] Would it not be enough for the principles of theology to be admitted as evident by God, since these principles are received on the basis of his testimony? Also, why mention the link of subordination to the "science of the blessed"?

We can, perhaps, distinguish two reasons. The first would come from the humanly scientific nature of theology. As such, theology supposes that the truths on which its reasoning is based would be truths not for God alone, but also for man—that is, truths that are capable of being evident to man. This evidence cannot be reached by man in the present life, but can be reached in the future life, in his vision of God. Without this, faith would not be capable of establishing the continuity between the transcendental evidence of divine science and that of faith, which, as imperfect understanding, presupposes a perfect state of understanding of these truths.

This leads us to the second reason, which gives their full meaning to both faith and theological investigation. In fact, if we bear in mind that faith has an inherent obscurity, we can understand that human intelligence can bear this obscurity only if it is provisional. The same is true of theological conclusions. The light of theological conclusions validates understanding and makes it capable of appropriating the clarity that is there to be understood, diffused in the obscurity of faith. But theological conclusions do not diminish the darkness of faith itself; this light of theology stems from that which bathes the understanding of the blessed but also, irresistibly, draws the spirit of the believer toward the fullness of clarity that is promised to him. Theological science—here, on this earth—is a participation in the theology of the blessed, as it is an actual communion with those who enjoy the state of blessedness, and is a sort of first fruit of its promised possession.

A legitimate extension of the notion of subalternation leads us to say that, in the believer, theology is subalternate to the science of vision which one day will be conceded to it. In this vision the theologian will find the definitive answer to all the questions posed by faith, which have formed the subject of his investigation. All the efforts of his believing reason will have produced only incomplete replies to these questions, true but deceptive, and only provisionally satisfying. But all this will have given rise to a more and more acute longing for vision in the theologian himself. However high a level scientific theology should be placed on, it is forced to exist in an incurable state of imperfection in this life. This imperfection generates dissatisfaction and healthy impatience. The object toward which theological investigation bends its whole dynamism is the beatific vision.[22]

It has been necessary to go more deeply into the thought of St. Thomas Aquinas in order to compare his understanding of the science of theology with Gutiérrez's view of Thomas' thought. From what we have seen, can we say that the essential element of St. Thomas' thought on theology as a science consists in considering it the fruit of the encounter of faith and reason? In one sense, one can reply in the affirmative, but in another sense, and as Gutiérrez understands it, the answer has to be no. In effect, we are dealing with a meeting between faith and reason, but this meeting brings consequences for theology that Gutiérrez is not prepared to consider and to which, furthermore, he is opposed.

Some claim to find in this work "an effort to bring faith and life together to reconcile them." We have seen the need for unity, hierarchy, and order in theological concepts if the light of theology is to lead us to a better understanding of the mysteries. It is a question of construction and organization. The plan of the *Summa* itself is proof of this. Scientific theology leads to a "system," to a logically structured whole, that follows a plan in which the different elements are diversified as stemming from principles that more or less explicitly rule the key points of the construction and its dispositions. This systematization is the normal and beneficial consequence of this understanding of faith which exercises its reasoning powers on this process in accord with the requirements of the human mind, which always seeks unity.[23] This is precisely what St. Thomas says in articles 3 and 7 of the first question of the *Summa:* "utrum Sacra Doctrina sit una" (a 3). If one reads the body of the article and the replies to the objections, one cannot fail to appreciate St. Thomas' understanding of the unity of theology and its systematization:

Ad primum ergo dicendum quod sacra doctrina non determinat de Deo et de creaturis ex aequo: sed de Deo principaliter et de creaturis secundum quod *referuntur a Deo,* ut at principium vel finem. Unde *unitas* scientiae non impeditur [I, q. 1, a 3, ad/um].

Omnia autem pertractantur in sacra doctrina sub ratione Dei: vel quia sunt ipse Deus; vel quia habent *ordinem ad Deum,* ut ad principium et finem [I, q. 1, a 7, corpus].

Omnia alia quae determinantur in sacra doctrina, comprehenduntur sub Deo: non ut partes vel species vel accidentia, sed ut *ordinata* aliqualiter ad ipsum [I, q. 1, a 7 ad 2 um.]

Now it is precisely this need for systematization that Gutiérrez considers "a degradation of the thomistic concept of theology," arising in Scholastic theology after the thirteenth century. This is another example of his failure to state both sides of a case. What he is going to criticize is the reduction of theology to the need for systematization and clear exposition. But there are two points here, and it is not clear whether he proposes to criticize the reduction or the systematization. We have seen that systematization is essential for St. Thomas. Gutiérrez's intention becomes clearer a little later when he says that "scholastic theology will thus gradually become, especially after the Council of Trent, an ancillary discipline of the *magisterium* of the Church. Its function will be '(1) to define, present and explain revealed truths; (2) to examine doctrine, to denounce and condemn false doctrines, and to defend true ones; (3) to teach revealed truths authoritatively.' "[24]

Can it be that the definition of truths is not an operation essential to theological reasoning, as understood by St. Thomas? The work of theological reasoning is carried on through precise elaboration of definitions, through going deeper than their formal content, analyzing, classifying, dividing, making distinctions, and all the other operations that tend to organize, if only in a descriptive fashion, the content of the word of God and of Christian life, which brings the word of God into being within humanity.[25]

We are evidently not dealing with a dogmatic definition. For St. Thomas, definition meant placing oneself in front of the word of God, in the "lectio" of it. The texts were commentated with a progressive penetration that started with the grammar and logic and proceeded to the *sense,* unearthing it through a first conceptual elaboration. Then one reached the doctrine that lies beyond the text, thanks to a quest for the internal relationships of the thought and its implied concepts. Then came the "quaestio," then the "disputatio." To omit this definitive aspect of St. Thomas Aquinas' theology is to remove an essential part of theological science as he conceived it.

Gutiérrez also classes the explanation of revealed truths as belonging to a later epoch and as a "degradation of the thomistic concept of theology." One has to read only a little of St. Thomas to realize the importance he attached to the connection of mysteries among themselves and to the role of analogy in reaching an explanation of revealed truths.[26] What is science in general, if not a search for a new understanding, or rather a new way of understanding something? If we omit this aspect, what is left of theology?

Gutiérrez also considers that "to examine doctrine, to denounce and condemn false doctrines, and to defend true ones" is another form of this later "degradation of the thomistic concept of theology." It is clear that the theologian has a different function from the ecclesiastical magisterium, however closely they are related. Theology has its own laws, proper to the service of the word of God in the Church, not only in order to understand it better but also to defend it through this understanding. Surely St. Thomas replies in the affirmative when asked "if theology is argumentative"! (Iq, Ia, 7).

Gutiérrez's account of what is permanent in the thought of St. Thomas on theology "as a rational science" amounts, I claim, to an evaporation of "the science of theology." For him, systematization is not permanent, and neither is clear exposition; explanation of truths is not permanent, neither is the aspect of being an ancillary discipline to the ecclesiastical magisterium; the examination of doctrines is not permanent, nor is the teaching of true ones and the denunciation of false ones. All this, he claims, stems from later than the thirteenth century and, above all, from the Council of Trent. He claims that there are "permanent and indispensable functions of all theological thinking," but asks that they be rescued from "the division and defamation they have suffered throughout history." What must especially be retained, he claims, is "a reflective outlook and style."

So what is left of theology? What is the "reflective style" of St. Thomas that must be retained? Is it not perhaps the "scientific" style? In his attempts to "demythologize" theology, has Gutiérrez not achieved its complete evaporation? At least, there is nothing left of the theology of St. Thomas. If, besides all this, theology has to renounce the service offered it by philosophy in favor of that of the "social, psychological and biological sciences," can one find any trace of St. Thomas' concept of theology?

We know that St. Thomas made philosophy the preferred instrument of his theological reflection. Also, theology's need for philosophy is obvious. There was no need to wait for the Middle Ages to introduce the philosophical notions of substance, nature, person, or sign into theology, and even into its dogmatic formulations. It could not have been otherwise, since revelation itself uses the words, images, and notions that had been worked out by man on the basis of his experience. Theological reflection deals primarily with these notions; and to understand what God has tried to tell us, to reach a certain understanding of the mystery, a study of the language God used to speak to man is indispensable. This language is directed to all men and discovers his reality to them, as well as that of the world in its deepest and most essential aspect—that is, in its relationship to God, the supreme reality and principle of all reality. It is not a philosophical language, but it is impossible to understand its meaning without the help of philosophy, whose object is precisely the understanding of all that is deepest and most universal in reality.[27]

We have said that theology uses philosophy as a necessary instrument; therefore, if philosophy is an instrument of theology in its theological work, in the act of theologizing, theology has thereby chosen the rational instrument it needs. Therefore, it has to be alert to the world of ideas to see what human thought can offer it, but not all the different currents of thought will be equally apt for a greater understanding of the mysteries of God. The most up-to-date current of thought will not always be the best instrument for theology. It is in this sense and only in this sense, of being bound up in theological work, that philosophy is the "handmaid of theology."

It is worth remarking that however necessary the help that theology receives from philosophy, theology does not depend on philosophy, though there are theologians today who would wish it so.[28] Seeing philosophy as something that expresses man's being and the idea he has of himself at every stage of the development of culture, these theologians would have theology make the philosophy of their time its own and use it to understand revealed truth. Gutiérrez is in this line of theologians when he tells us that the meeting between faith and reason should not be tied to any one philosophy. This definition of theology as "a meeting between faith and reason, not exclusively between faith and any one philosophy," could mean that theology does not depend on any one philosophy but that it can choose the one it needs. If so, I would agree. Or it could mean that this meeting can come about by picking and choosing a particular philosophy. In this case I would disagree, since this leads to the view that the assumption of a "present day" philosophy can profoundly modify the interpretation of revealed truth as this has been understood in the Church. The basis these theologians claim as justification for this change of hermeneutics can be expressed as follows: Can the word of God be understood independently of the man to whom it is directed?

Theology cannot be dependent on philosophy, because it is entirely dependent on the word of God. Its vocation is to scrutinize an object far beyond the reach of all philosophical investigation, since theology is a mystery that cannot be known except through divine revelation. It is known by human reason, indeed, but by a reason that has accepted instruction by faith and has been raised above itself, above all the objects that remain natural to it, raised to the level of the thought of God himself. If theology has need of philosophy, it is because it needs to use human proceedings of investigation and knowledge to reach its superhuman object; but what theology seeks lies beyond all the natural objectives of human investigation. Theology can seek a greater understanding of these truths only because theological reasoning has received these truths in faith. In this sense, and within these limits only, can philosophy be a servant of theology. Philosophy can serve only when it is taken into the theological task, since, on its own level, philosophy remains independent.[29]

If philosophy is to serve theology, this does not mean that any philosophy will be as useful as another as an instrument of theological knowledge; theology has to choose the appropriate instrument.[30] How is it to set about making a choice? Obviously, it cannot use a philosophy whose metaphysics is false and defies common sense. Equally obviously, "common sense" here does not necessarily mean what is generally recognized by men; it means an immediate understanding of first principles that are evident in themselves.[31] Furthermore, "any philosophy that claims to serve as a conceptual instrument of faith should appear as a synthesis of notions and judgments based on a concept that is wide enough to unite a great number of aspects of reality under its banner. The broader this concept the deeper and more illuminating will the philosophy tied to it be."[32]

In this sense, the only ideas that are capable of supporting an authentic philosophy are those that transcend all particular categories of worldly reality and are therefore called transcendental. These ideas are being, essence, unity, goodness, truth, and beauty. All forms and shares of reality can be reduced to them and, in their light, can take on an organic elucidation, opening infinite perspectives to the human mind. Among these transcendental ideas, that of being is the foremost, since the others are aspects of the idea of being. Being cannot be the enemy of any reality. A fundamental analysis of being in relation to reality—elaborating the concepts of our science in accord with the requirements of reality, open to the analogy of transcendental ideas, and following the outlines of what exists with docility and obedience—will be capable of penetrating the innermost essence of things and communicating it intelligibly, without in any way destroying their originality, unity, and particularity.

While it is true that Vatican II encourages us to take "contemporary philosophies" into account and to "hold on to what is true in them," it also invites us to scrutinize the final principles behind them in order to discover what is false in them, on the basis of a "philosophical patrimony that is valid forever."[33]

Therefore, if theology needs a realistic philosophy, a philosophy of transcendental ideas, and above all one of being, perceived and encapsulated with all the richness of analogy, what can we say of a theology that would abandon philosophy, not believing it necessary? Can the change of approach that Gutiérrez offers, that is, to prefer sociology to the wide horizons of philosophical wisdom, really be an ideal instrument of theological reasoning? I do not think so. Nor did St. Thomas, who frequently spoke of the difference between the sciences of the *quia* and the *propter quid*. Those of the *quia* do not give a broad and deep explanation of reality.[34] If we are seeking a better understanding of the plan of love offered by God to man, and, primarily, of the fact that this plan is presented through a revelation to which man ascends through faith, surely it cannot be sociology alone that defines man? Do we not need a philosophical and metaphysical knowledge of man as well?

If we consider that even a philosophy of liberty, for example, seems too narrow a systematization, surely this is even more true of sociology, psychology, or biology? A philosophy that is centered and built on the idea of liberty leaves too many aspects of real existence out of account. This is the situation in which, for example, Sartre found himself in *L'être et le néant* , in which he felt himself incapable of giving a metaphysical explanation of the origin of the world.

Sociology or psychology must necessarily be even narrower; so any system that is built on such a basis must be extremely precarious. The sociological viewpoint leaves many aspects of reality out of account. How, then, can Gutiérrez's proposal to substitute philosophy by sociology, in order to make the latter the representative of reason, which goes out to meet faith in order to produce theological reasoning, be productive? What light is reason, represented by sociology, capable of shedding on the mystery of the Resurrection?[35]

This limitation of sociology does not deny its usefulness and the service it can lend to theology; it means metaphysics cannot be supplanted by the social, psychological, and biological sciences.

Conclusion

Our conclusion to this lengthy consideration of the "classic tasks" of theology, as presented by Gustavo Gutiérrez, is that in his attempt to purify these tasks from all the accretions of history he empties theology of its content. What is left of theology as wisdom? Has he not described its history as consisting of "meditation on the Bible geared toward spiritual growth" and told us that it is "above all monastic and therefore characterized by a spiritual life removed from worldly concern"? Can he really suggest that such a theology is useful at a time when, according to *Gaudium et Spes,* the Church is addressing herself to the world?

After his run through fourteen centuries of theology as wisdom, it is only logical that he should look with great expectations to a "new way of doing theology," and yet he claims that theology as wisdom must remain "a permanent dimension of theology." The same emptying process can be seen at work in his consideration of theology as rational knowledge.

My own theological studies in the tradition and spirit of St. Thomas Aquinas enable me to see that the author of *A Theology of Liberation* knows very little of St. Thomas, who would never recognize his thought in Gutiérrez's summary of it. According to Gutiérrez, theology has come to be an encounter between faith and sociology, as the latter seems to be the qualified representative of reason. There is no longer any need for functions, systems, order, hierarchy, and unity, nor is there need for any connection with the mysteries, nor for analogy, nor for metaphysics as the representative and function of reason in theology's meeting with faith. What, then, is left?

Why does he tell us that its function as rational knowledge should be permanent? We find the same irony as in the preceding section. What he is in fact doing is preparing the way for his "new way of doing theology." This is how he presents the theology that is supposed to provide a theological future for Latin America.

So much, then, for his view of the past of theology. He then turns to the present and, in the central section of the first chapter of his book, examines theology as critical reflection on praxis; and it is this section that I propose to examine in the next two chapters. He divides his section into two subsections: historical praxis and critical reflection. I will devote a chapter to each and will end with a short consideration of his conclusion.

To discuss theology as a critical reflection on praxis is to discuss something that "has gradually become more clearly defined in recent years," Gutiérrez claims, and it is perhaps the novelty of this section, as he sees it, that leads him to be sparse in his references to other present-day authors. This suggests that the notion of theology as critical reflection on praxis is clear; but we shall see whether it really is.

Chapter 4
Theology as "Historical Praxis"

One looks in vain for a precise definition of what the author means by this phrase, "historical praxis." "It is as though the words Praxis and History exercise such a fascination in themselves that one can dispense with inquiry into their meaning," writes Cottier.[1] These pages (6–11) of Gutiérrez's book are an account of the factors that justify "a new way of doing theology," rather than a definition of what should be understood by "historical praxis." Something of his meaning of "historical praxis" comes through from the context in which the phrase is used, but changes in the context multiply the possible meanings of the expression, or at least its shades of meaning.

Let us proceed directly to a study of the different factors, although one must recognize that it is methodologically incorrect to study factors that contribute to making something that is not defined. It would be all right if, after studying all the factors, we were told what "historical praxis" is, but such is not the case in this work. However, the discussion of "critical reflection" will shed more light on the subject.

In chapter 1, between pages 16 and 18, I set out the factors that Gutiérrez considers in this section. Schematically speaking, there are ten of them, and I propose to analyze each in turn and then proceed to a synthesis. Inevitably, this will lead to repetition, since the same matter will be dealt with several times, although from different viewpoints. We can claim that, as Gutiérrez says, these factors will underline "the existential and active aspects of the Christian life."

37

Charity and Faith

"*Charity* has been fruitfully rediscovered as the centre of the Christian life," Gutiérrez tells us. This, he then says, has led to a more biblical view of faith as "an act of trust, a going out of oneself, a commitment to God and neighbour, a relationship with others. . . . This is the foundation of the *praxis* of the Christian, of his active presence in history."[2]

Let us examine this first factor very carefully, because it is of supreme importance. It deals with the primacy of charity, with the connection between faith and charity, and with these two virtues as the basis of the active presence of the Christian in history. These three affirmations are extremely important, both in themselves and in Gutiérrez's work.

In what sense is charity the center of the Christian life? A full treatise on the meaning of charity in Christian life is impossible here, but it is certain that charity is above all the love of God for us in Christ (Rom 8:39). This love, diffused in us by the Holy Spirit, becomes ours and makes us capable of loving with the same quality of love as that possessed by God himself. Consequently, the Holy Spirit, who engenders divine life in the baptized, leads them to love the Father with a love which is, if not equal to, at least of the same nature as his; it enables them to live—in a way—on a divine level and to live with him in a true society (Eph 1:4). Christians are "those who love God" (1 Cor 2:9, Rom 8:28) with a love of gratitude and religious fervor (Rom 5:5). In the same way that the profession of faith is impossible without the light of the Holy Spirit (1 Cor 12:3) and in the same way that it is the Spirit who makes us grow in hope (Rom 15:3), it is the Spirit who makes us love divinely by revealing to the sons the treasures of the love in the heart of their Father:

> What God has prepared for those who love him, God has
> revealed to us through the Spirit, for the Spirit searches

everything, even the depths of God. For what person
knows a man's thoughts except the spirit of the man which
is in him? So also no one comprehends the thoughts of
God except the spirit of God. Now we have received not
the spirit of the world but the Spirit which is from God
that we might understand the gifts bestowed on us by God
[1 Cor 2:9–12].

The gift that sums up all the others is the gift of the beloved
Son (Rom 8:32). In this way the Spirit shows the believer the
infinity of charity supposed by the suffering on the cross and, in
a way, sets the Christian on Calvary. The Lord had told his
apostles that the Holy Spirit would teach them to understand
him properly (Jn 14:16, 15:26, 16:13–14). It is in the light of the
Holy Spirit that the Christian grasps divine love in the Passion
of Jesus; nothing can henceforth separate him from it (Rom
8:39), "for the love of Christ controls us" (2 Cor 5:14). So it is
the love of Christ, who sacrificed himself for us, that engenders
love for him in the believer. Our love for God and his Son is
always dependent on the love they have for us. In the light of
the Holy Spirit, the Christian comes to understand this gratuitousness and from it draws the practical consequences that
orientate his life and decide his fidelity. Charity, born of the
contemplation of Christ crucified, then invades his whole soul
and determines both his desires and his acts: "The life I now live
in the flesh I live by faith in the Son of God who loved me and
gave himself for me" (Gal 2:20).

Since the charity infused by the Holy Spirit is the same love
of God and of Christ, the Christian who lives in Christ is impelled to love his brothers as God and Christ love them (Eph
5:1–2). So charity, in the sense of love for one's neighbor,
becomes the characteristic that unites the sons with their Father
in heaven.

The example of Jesus shows that this love should extend to
the total gift of oneself, in a sense a consecration: "through love
the servants of one another" (Gal 5:13), exactly as the Lord was
(Mt 6:24). This love is a sort of debt because it is the practical

way of showing God the gratitude that is owed to him for his very gifts. In one sole act of service to one's neighbor, the Christian loves and helps his brother, loves God, and offers him a spiritual sacrifice of thanksgiving.

There are not, therefore, two virtues of charity but one alone, and the two objects of this charity—God and our neighbor— although different from one another, and with their own order and hierarchy, cannot be dissociated from one another. To exclude even one man from this love would be to exclude Christ himself, who died for all men and who offers the Father's love to all; but we have to ask whether this means that loving one's neighbor is exactly the same as loving God. Through charity the human person commits himself totally to a personal Being—the divine Persons—who is situated so far beyond what we can see, hear, touch, or feel that the human person cannot experience even his own love with any certainty. Should it not therefore be the neighbor who represents God for us, and is not loving one's neighbor the way to love God?[3]

This is not precisely what Scripture tells us, but it does say that love of the neighbor, whom we can see, is a sign of authenticity in our love for God, whom we cannot see (1 Jn 3:10). Our neighbor is not God, and if he can lead us to God, this is because this neighbor is loved because of God. If our neighbor is loved for himself, he will hold to and remain in our love for him. This is not something to be censured, but it should not be confused with love of God. Our neighbor leads us to God only when we see in him a sign of the hidden God, who is to be loved above all things, and beyond the neighbor's own value as a person, which entitles him to be loved. Our neighbor can lead us to God only if we love God, in himself, above all things—if we love God in all that we love.[4]

Surely the mystery of Christ can tell us something on this point? God became man; infinite love became incarnate in a heart of man. The response of our love to God is directed to Christ, and in him and through him we can rise to the height of the divinity. The neighbor's role consists in continuing the human presence of Christ, in order to beg for the heart of the Christian and awaken him from his stupor. It is Christ, in our neighbor, who asks for our care, love, commitment, service, and compassion. So to pass our neighbor by is to pass by Christ, the sacrament of God (cf. 1 Jn 3:17).

Clearly, this can be known, let alone lived, only in faith. Seeing Christ in our neighbor and loving our neighbor because of this is an act of faith, of faith operating through charity (Gal 5:6). In this way there is no reason to confuse love of our neighbor, a love that is charity, an obligatory prolongation or extension of the love of God, with a love of man that is based on human solidarity. This human love is in itself noble and is indeed the principle of the great undertakings of this world, but it is limited. It cannot claim the universality of charity and, above all, it is not based on unity of all men in Christ, all of whom are called to participate in the life of God.

If charity lies behind all works of mercy toward our neighbor, this is because Christ, who is loved, continues suffering and lacking so many things and so many basic rights in the person of his members, especially the poor and dispossessed; but just like Christ, what the Christian wants above all and in the first place, as much for himself as for his brothers, is union in the life of God. I say "above all"; but this does not mean that the temporal needs of man should be minimized in importance, let alone forgotten. On the contrary, these needs are perceived in the light of faith as a symbol and embodiment of his spiritual needs. Temporal poverty becomes an occasion for the application not only of active mercy but a feeling of mercy. This feeling can have a higher object, but it has to go through the temporal if it is not to founder in unreality. Understood in this way, love of our neighbor, far from being a substitute for the love of God, draws its meaning and strength from this love. It is true that the Christian loves God in loving his brothers, but he loves his brothers because he loves God, and he loves God more than his brothers, more than himself.

Since love of one's neighbor is the most easily controlled,

although its motivation may continue to be mysterious, it has been given to us as a sign of the love of God, of whose love it is the effect and visible part. Loving God through one's neighbor, loving one's neighbor in God, is a single movement of the heart, inspired by charity. It is a single response, with various manifestations, to "the great love with which he loves us" (Eph 2:4).

If we now return to Gutiérrez, who tells us "charity has been fruitfully rediscovered as the centre of the Christian life," we are entitled to ask in what sense he understands this. Is it in taking stock of the value of charity, as I have tried to present it? Or is it, on the other hand, a question of "rediscovering" that charity is synonymous, without further ado and without further distinction, with the love of man for man by virtue of human solidarity and with no hierarchy in the goods given to him? St. Thomas speaks of the preeminence, for various reasons, of the communication of the goods of the spirit over the goods of the body.[5]

Again, what concept of charity has our author in mind when he speaks of its rediscovery as a recent emphasis that is different from its emphasis in the immediate past? Or, to put the question another way, is he talking about the rediscovery of divine love as described by St. John—of, that is, God's love as directed to the sinner, which tends to make him someone worthy of love, a friend of God, who is capable of giving back to God love for love?[6]

God claims the reciprocity of man's love and therefore bases it in true intercommunion (Jn 14:21-23, 15:4). God intends to make men truly his Son's friends and brothers of Christ and, because of this, to bind them closely one to another in a bond of brotherhood that owes its origin to the very mystery of the Trinity. Deep dialogue among men is not possible without the dialogue of men with God.

If we are talking of rediscovering charity in this sense—that is, including a communion, a reciprocity, a true friendship from which friendship toward other men stems—we must emphasize the aspect of knowledge of God: "No longer do I call you servants, for the servant does not know what his master is doing; but I have called you friends for all that I have heard from my Father I have made known to you" (Jn 15:14–15). Whatever form knowledge of God takes, it cannot come about outside revelation and faith until we come to the immediate vision of God. The word of God, the only source of supernatural knowledge, can come to us only through faith; there can be no means other than knowledge of entering into the depths of God. It is true, however, that the ways of pure knowledge are insufficient and end by deceiving us. We also need longing for God, love and affectivity, but the factor of affectivity does not contradict understanding, nor is it a parallel process; rather, love comes to complete and enrich the understanding of God. Love does not come to replace understanding. However different the affective movements may appear from understanding, or however superior the power of union implicit in love may appear, its autonomy is not such that affectivity can be studied without recognizing a dependence of love on knowledge at the outset. Affectivity presupposes understanding and results from it. With regard to the life of God and his decree of love for man, this understanding is faith. Charity presupposes faith.[7]

Faith

Since there is an intimate connection between charity and faith, as we have seen and as Gutiérrez expressly declares, let us see what he tells us about faith. Examination of his concept of biblical faith will help us better to understand his concept of charity, which he sees as a major factor influencing the "new way of doing theology" in Latin America. He defines the biblical view of the faith as "an act of trust, a going out of oneself, a commitment to God and neighbour, a relationship with others." In this sense, he claims, St. Paul tells us that faith works through charity: "Love is the nourishment and the fullness of faith, the gift of oneself to the Other and invariably to others"

The question that needs asking here is whether this description of the faith does not omit the notional cognitive aspect.[8]

When St. John speaks of "believing," of the act of faith, he is always thinking of the commitment that brings one to be a disciple of the Lord by virtue of a decision that has to be irrevocable. This decision supposes trust in Jesus, but there is a difference between different types of trust. True believers are those who "decide" for Christ, who trust in him, who take him for himself, as he is.[9]

The expression "to believe in the name" does not mean only "to believe in the person," as if the "name" were a simple Semitism to designate the person; it means adhering to the person but, at the same time, fully recognizing what this "name" (which is not defined) expresses. The Jews believed in Jesus merely as a worker of signs and miracles, sent by God. This was their characteristic "faith," which Jesus was to reject. The faith he required is perfect faith, believing in the "name" of the only Son of God, for which it is necessary to believe that Jesus is the only Son of the Father and to follow him, inasmuch as he is the Son and was sent by the Father.[10] Thus even when faith is considered as an act of trust in God, faith in Christ still supposes bearing the truth of the mystery of his Person in mind. A commitment to Christ supposes having accepted him as Son of God. For St. John, believing means "receiving the Word"; trust in Christ is abortive if it does not lead to revelation.

According to John, faith in Christ, in its perfect state, implies adherence to his message. One has to believe that Jesus is the Messiah (11:27, 20:31), the one who is sent by the Father (11:42, 17:8–21), the Son of God (20:31), who is sent from the dwelling place of the Father (16:27–30), who is in the Father (14:10–11), who alone has the right to say absolutely "I am" (8:24, 13:19). But the revelation of Jesus is not concerned only with him. Who sees him sees the Father (14:9), who listens to him has knowledge of the heavenly things that the Son has seen and heard concerning the Father in the inaccessible world of heaven (3:12–13, 6:18, 8:23). In this way Jesus presents us with a living and true God whom he alone can reveal.[11]

Jesus transmitted his words, the words the Father gave him, to the apostles (Jn 17:8) so that, thanks to his preaching, the world would know that the Father has sent him (17:23) out of love (3:16, 17–23). The Spirit will be charged with reminding them of all that Jesus told them (14:26). It would be useless for the Spirit to be charged with this task of reminding them of everything if the words of Jesus played a merely incidental part in his mission.

Faith, therefore, implies openness to the teaching of Christ, to his doctrine, at the same time as self-abandonment to his Person. If the doctrine is not preserved, the act of faith is deprived of one of its essential elements. To take the act of faith as pure trust leaves believers in ignorance of the truth; considering it as assent alone deprives them of the rock on which their certainties rest. The more confidence one has in Jesus, the more his teaching will reach into one's heart; while the words of Jesus take deepest root in the hearts of those who listen to him, confidence in Christ grows; therefore men are invited to give their whole being to Christ. This total giving of oneself implies handing over one's intelligence, as well as one's heart.

If we now return to Gutiérrez's concept of biblical faith as "an act of trust, a going out of oneself, a commitment to God and neighbour, a relationship with others," we cannot fail to see that this notion of faith, which he considers adequate, lacks an essential element that must be taken into account: understanding the mystery, with all that the word supposes. It is true that he tells us: "According to the Bible, faith is the total response of man to God, who saves through love"; but what does he understand by "total response"? He goes on to define it for us: "In this light the understanding of the faith appears as the understanding, not of the simple affirmation—almost memorization—of truths, but of a commitment, an overall attitude, a particular posture toward life."

The understanding of faith—that is, theology—is an understanding not of a simple affirmation of truths but of a commit-

ment, an overall attitude. The objection I make to this simple
form of approaching both faith and theology is this: are there
not other aspects of faith that come between a simple affirmation
of truths and an overall attitude to life? St. Thomas Aquinas,
speaking of faith as virtue, takes the trouble to distinguish between the object of faith, the inner act of faith, the outer act of
faith, and finally the virtue of faith considered in itself.[12] In view
of this and in view of what we have seen about faith in the Bible,
what place do the truths revealed by Christ, and Christ himself
as revealed truth, come to occupy? What is the object of faith?
If not the truths, is the object of faith an attitude to life? Is it
not perhaps true that the Christian has an attitude to life because he has believed in Someone and because he has believed
something? Faith, as our author shows it to us, has no "object,"
no content. His notion of faith does not concord with the biblical
notion.

The consequences of this notion for theology, as understanding of faith, are very serious. According to Gutiérrez, theology
would be "the understanding . . . of an overall attitude, a particular posture toward life." This leads him into an unavoidable
contradiction, when later he defines theology according to the
new mode in which he would have us see it:

> Theological reflection would then necessarily be a criti-
> cism of society and the Church insofar as they are called
> and addressed by the Word of God; it would be a critical
> theory worked out in the light of the Word, accepted in
> faith, inspired by a practical purpose—and therefore in-
> dissolubly linked to historical praxis.[13]

According to this, theology judges society and the Church in
the light of the word accepted in faith, but earlier he told us that
faith is commitment, attitude, a particular posture toward life.
Perhaps he could object that this is not exactly what he said,
that what he is opposed to is the understanding of theology as
a "simple affirmation . . . of truths," but then one can ask

whether theology is or is not an understanding of the mysteries of God. Although the wisdom function and theology's task of being rational knowledge should abide (we have already seen on what a reduced level), Gutiérrez thinks that it is reflection of praxis that redefines the other tasks.[14]

The faith that Gutiérrez proposes is certainly not the faith of the Bible, and this is why his theology lacks doctrinal content, however much he holds back from declaring this in so many words.

The Historical Evolution of Spirituality

This is the next factor in preparing the "new way of doing theology," the theology of liberation. I must confess that, here again, I am disappointed by the author's lack of scientific inquiry. It is very difficult to debate with someone who manipulates the history of spirituality to his own ends in this way. In a series of rapid jumps and imprecise quotes he takes aspects that suit his thesis and tries to give the impression of mastering fields of knowledge that, in fact, he only touches upon. His gallop through the history of spirituality that leads to "the spirituality of the activity of the Christian in the world" tries to impose a system on history that it will not bear. His flight over the centuries becomes a challenge to historical truth. Take, for example, his negative two-line conclusion on the value of hermitical and monastic life, which he sees as characterized by "withdrawal from the world"; but St. Benedict asked those who called at the monastery door whether they were "truly seeking God." This is not a withdrawal but a special way of seeking God. We have already seen that Gutiérrez could be expected to give a negative and rather unobjective view of monastic life from his remarks on the wisdom function of theology as it was practiced in the monasteries. He refers to René Bultot and his work on the theme of "contempt for the world."[15] Bultot's tendentious interpretation was in fact vigorously contested by various writers in a special number of the *Revue d'ascétique et mystique.*

[10] In these articles, many mistakes about the monastic life in its aspects of "withdrawal, flight, contempt for the world" are rectified. As the late Cardinal Daniélou notes: "Despising the world is not the same thing as preferring God to the world."[17]

Is there perhaps something wrong in affirming, as Cassian did, that the goods of this world are only relative values? In no way. This does not in any way mean that these values are to be despised in themselves but only that the bad use the monk could make of them was to be condemned.[18] If the phrase "withdrawal from the world" can lead to misunderstanding, so can that other phrase of which Gutiérrez is so fond, "activity in the world." Both need precision in use, which is lacking in this work.

What Gutiérrez is trying to tell us in this section is that there is a process that follows a straight line from the contemplative life to "activity in the world." In support of this, for example, he says: "Viewed historically, this stage [of the mendicant orders] can be considered as a transition to Ignatian spirituality, which sought a difficult but fruitful synthesis between contemplation and action." It seems to me that the mere fact that Ignatian spirituality is chronologically later than Dominican spirituality does not necessarily mean that the latter is a form of transition toward the former. Or does Gutiérrez mean to imply that a religious order approaches his ideal only by advancing toward "the spirituality of the activity of the Christian in the world"?[19]

I absolutely agree with all efforts to work out a genuine spirituality of the lay state, but I am not convinced that it is either necessary or convenient—or according to God's plan—to minimize religious life in general in order to do so. Nor is it acceptable to claim a basic mutation in the finality and spirituality of each religious order. For our author, it would appear that the religious order that is most deeply involved in the "world" has to occupy the best place in the process of advancement toward what he considers the ideal: "the activity of the Christian in the world."

To know what is understood by "world," to distinguish the

true activity in this "world" that belongs to the lay state from what belongs to the religious, is a difficult matter, and we have only affirmations full of superficiality and equivocation on these themes. In what way can it be said that this vision of the history of spirituality is a contributory factor to the "new way of doing theology," which he is going to present to us? One can suspect that if "activity" has a preeminent place, a theology of "praxis" will have to occupy the same preeminence. But how clear is this preeminence, when we are not given a precise definition of what is meant by "world" or what is meant by "activity"?

Anthropological Aspects of Revelation

I agree absolutely with Gutiérrez when he says that "today there is a greater sensitivity to the anthropological aspects of revelation"; but what should we understand by "aspects"? And if we bear these "aspects" in mind, what valid conclusions can we come to that are relevant to a "new way of doing theology"? With regard to the first question, what does it mean to be sensitive to the "anthropological aspects of revelation"? A modern theologian who has devoted much time and attention to this is Karl Rahner,[20] but this is not the place to enter into a discussion of this thought (which is accepted by many though criticized by some). We can only say that it is fundamental for a good understanding of these "anthropological aspects of revelation."

In contemplating the mysteries of faith in theology it is essential to make the relation between these mysteries and man clear, without thereby reducing revelation and its content to the existential experience of man. One has to show how the events through which God has spoken to us always contain an affirmation about God and about man, and in this sense I agree with Gutiérrez's statement. The logic of this statement leads to the conclusion that it is the mystery of God that reveals the sense and meaning for man. Will he be able to follow this logic with his exposition of theology as critical reflection? Or, on the other hand, will man and his reasoned reflection on himself—without intervention from the light of faith in contact with the word—impose the meaning and content of the gospel and revelation? One can never elude the web of relationships between the natural and the supernatural orders.

At this stage we must ask in what way a "greater sensitivity to the anthropological aspects of revelation," as we understand the phrase, can be a factor in the new theological approach that Gutiérrez intends to show us. If it is revelation or "the Gospel message"—as Gutiérrez admits—that "reveals us to ourselves in our situation before the Lord and other men," we have to know this revelation thoroughly, and this supposes specific teaching. Now this specific teaching, in faith as in theology, is precisely what disappears from Gutiérrez's approach. We shall see this more clearly later.

There is another way of being "sensitive" to the anthropological aspects of revelation, and we must be careful to bear it in mind; this is to reflect on *Christian belief* and the benefit it can bring men. This, in turn, supposes full knowledge of the revealed data and, also, profound knowledge of man himself, which can be attained only through a true philosophy.

Now the trouble is that Gutiérrez has been trying to achieve progressive detachment from the data of revelation and from the philosophical riches proffered by the social sciences, which he takes as convenient representatives of reason in its meeting with faith. So, in this aspect as well, he places himself in a difficult situation, from which there is no way out, except by changing many of the presuppositions on which he bases his argument. By freeing himself from a particular metaphysics, he seems to be in danger of suffering all the tribulations of a subjectivism that will lead him to ideology.[21]

Still another way of being "sensitive" to the anthropological aspects of revelation is through correcting the errors in the thought of one's time while at the same time listening to what the world says. One of the most beneficial ways for man of doing this is to give him back his identity, which can be obscured by

ideological or philosophical error. It therefore becomes the task
of theology to clarify these deviations from the truth. Perhaps
this is a warning that Gutiérrez will take into account when he
comes to deal with the question of Marxism?

The Very Life of the Church

Another factor is the very life of the Church, which, he says,
"appears ever more clearly as a *locus theologicus.*" I have already noted the lack of precision in his reference to Chenu,
when he quotes him as writing of "the participation of Christians in the important social movements of their time," when in
fact Chenu was writing about the whole life of the church.[22]

The fact that the life of the Church is a source for all theological analysis is something the "new theology" first attempted to
show and has often called to mind thereafter. The way in which
Gutiérrez understands this is: "The Word of God gathers and
is incarnated in the community of faith which gives itself to the
service of all men." Gutiérrez adds something else: Since the
Church is not centered upon itself and finds itself in the "joys
and the hopes, the griefs and the anxieties of men of this age"
(*GS,* no. 1), this means that the presence and the activity of the
Church in the world become a starting point for theological
reflection.

We can see clearly how he is preparing "the new way of doing
theology" that he is going to offer us, and we can perhaps
synthesize his thought in a syllogism:

The Word of God is incarnate in the community of faith,
which is the Church.

But the Church is such insofar as it shares the joys and hopes
of men.

Therefore the Word of God is incarnate in this life of the
Church which finds itself in the joys and griefs of men.

Where does this lead? To the fact that, as he said before, the very life of the Church appears ever more clearly as a *"locus theologicus."*

He is making another approach, and this time through the life of the Church, as *locus theologicus,* to his "new way of doing theology." A *locus theologicus*—particularly in this case, when it is the very life of the Church—is always of great importance for theology. The life of the Church, presented as solidarity with the hopes and griefs of mankind, in this way becomes "a starting point for theological reflection." I think that if one submits this type of thinking to the laws of logic, its sophisms and oversimplification will soon become apparent.

I have already spoken of the frequency with which Gutiérrez makes selective quotes from Congar, Chenu, and others, but let us try to see a little more clearly why he simplifies Chenu's thought in this case. In its original context, the text he quotes refers to the whole of the life of the Church, which is wider than attention to the joys and griefs of humanity. Let us take another sentence of Chenu, slightly earlier than the text quoted by Gutiérrez, which he again takes out of its original context:

> But in faith the believer feels the onset and growth of a demanding appetite, an understanding of faith which with a lasting curiosity for the *revealed datum* provokes a religious and scientific appreciation of the disciplines that go to make it up: an immense field of source material that it would be presumptuous to reduce to a catalogue of propositions and a list of venerable texts, since the *"loci"* of the believer and the theologian are made up of the whole positive life of the Church, its customs and modes of thought, devotions and sacraments, its spiritualities, its institutions, its philosophies, in accordance with the handed-on catholicity of the faith in historical density and embracing the entire surface of civilizations.[23]

Perhaps the author of *A Theology of Liberation* could reply: Granted, that this social aspect is not the whole life of the Church; is it not at least an important element of this whole life and therefore a *locus theologicus,* just as the liturgy, say, or the magisterium of the Church? In reply to this I would say that since this would make it part of a living organism, this part has no life on its own, except as operating in its proper place and dependent on other parts of the organism, at least the basic ones. Now this is not what Gutiérrez is saying; for him, this part, on its own, would become the principal *locus theologicus.* Hence his attempt to present the wisdom and scientific functions of theology in such evaporated form; hence his concept of faith and charity; hence his presentation of centuries of spirituality, leading to activity in the world; hence his reticence with respect to revealed data, for which he always has a phrase that tends to lead us to separate our thought from what they are in reality, as well as from distortions; hence the frequent expressions: "transference away from attention to the being *per se* of supernatural realities," "the understanding not of the simple affirmation," "the goal is to balance and even to reject the primacy and almost exclusiveness which doctrine has enjoyed."

Gutiérrez speaks of the life of the Church as a *locus theologicus;* however, nowhere does he say that the Church cannot have life except as it is organized by the apostolic confession, the confession of a truth received from the Father through Jesus Christ, who is himself this truth. The apostolic succession puts us in direct touch with this truth, which is eschatogical, since it is eternal and yet appears in time, and enshrines all the riches of the mystery of the love of the Father.[24]

Gutiérrez says: "The Word of God gathers and is incarnated in the community of faith which gives itself to the service of all men"; but one must remember that the Incarnation has its own laws, laid down by God. The Word of God is incarnate in the Church only insofar as it is truly the Church—that is, the Church of tradition in the deep meaning of the word—only insofar as it transmits a truth in order to live from it, according to the requirements of this same truth. When Gutiérrez speaks of the Church as a "community of faith," what faith does he mean? What is the content of this faith? Talk of a *locus theologi-*

cus is common today; but its meaning must be seen in relation to the service it gives for the understanding of faith. The theologian obtains suitable arguments from these *loci;* he can also use them to prove his conclusions or to refute contrary ones. More important, however, is the fact that all *loci theologici* do not have the same value. Some produce irrefutable arguments, others mere probabilities; some, moreover, are proper to theology itself, while others belong to theological knowledge as though they came from "outside." The word of God in Scripture is the principal *locus,* not to say ultimately the only one. We must be very careful how we use language in defining *loci.* Praxis, for example, once it is proved to be a true *locus,* cannot claim the same primacy as revelation. We must be very careful not to identify praxis with the living tradition of the Church, which is precisely the confusion into which the author of *A Theology of Liberation* has fallen. We have noted this confusion in his treatment of the theme of "historical praxis."

The Signs of the Times

The next factor, the "signs of the times," is something that Gutiérrez says "can be characterized along the same lines," although, as he says, "this takes a step beyond narrow ecclesial limits." The general line of his thought is this: If the life of the Church is a *locus theologicus* and, as such, is influential in working out a "new way of doing theology," the "signs of the times" will also help in this working out, and they are found not only within the limits of the Church but in the world and in history. In note 29 he tells us that "despite its great interest, the notion of the signs of the times is far from being a clear and well-defined area. *Gaudium et Spes* does not attempt to define it; it only provides a description and some consequences for the life of faith." Whether or not there is a definition or description, our author should at least tell us in what sense he understands these "signs" if he is going to talk of them at all. One cannot speak of something and pass judgment on it without saying how one understands it, unless it is self-evident or at least well known to the intended audience. The "signs of the times" have no such self-evidence in theology.

Nevertheless, I think that even if the notion of the "signs of the times" has not been established with perfect clarity, it is not lacking in certain degrees of intelligibility about which one can speak. With particular reference to the theology of revelation, one can ask how far these degrees require a "new way of doing theology." In the first place, are there particular aspects that will help us to understand something of what is meant by these "signs of the times"? The expression, as Chenu says, "is one of the most meaningful phrases produced by the Council, and one that gives utterance to its basic preoccupations." This very significance should warn us against using the expression too facilely, since, in the mind of the Church of Vatican II, the expression has great resonance. What is at stake is the historicity of man as a being in the world.[25] Hence the importance of the expression and the seriousness with which it must be used.

Chenu, who has made a study of this theme, has traced its history in conformity with the place it occupies in the constitution on the Church in the world of today (nos. 4–10). The expression, clearly, is not one that has burst suddenly upon the theological scene, but it has a specific meaning when the temporal conjunctures in which the resources and faculties of nature unfold are studied, rather than nature itself in the abstract.[26] The encyclicals *Pacem in Terris* and *Ecclesiam Suam* used the phrase before *Gaudium et Spes,* and they identified certain aspects which mark what might be called the "signs of the times." With Chenu, one can say that the "signs of the times" are human phenomena whose subject matter is the relationship between the Church and the world and which are distinguished by their *openness* to the gospel. They are manifestations of evangelical values at work within the movements of history; without any doubt, they must be taken to include the emancipation of colonized peoples, the dignity of the human person, the promotion of cultural values and economic and social justice, the values of married life, etc. If one analyzes them more deeply, one can see, underlying them, the relationship between nature and grace, between secular history and the history of salvation. The error of identifying these two realities is as great as that of seeing them related only extrinsically, by chance or one on top of the other. This leads to the dualism in which "nature is considered in itself and grace as though it came from outside, with no secret understanding with nature and history."[27]

On the contrary, there are very close relationships between sacred and profane history, between nature and grace. For the believer, sacred and profane history are not two separate, parallel strands but are closely bound up with each other, and even tend toward the same end; but it is also true that they are not united by a process of cause and effect, in the sense that the building up of the world and human promotion can, by themselves, necessarily lead to the coming of the kingdom. On their own, neither history nor nature is capable of revealing the mystery of God; this can be done only by virtue of the word that comes from on high. The human promotion of man is not the same as his salvation, although my response to the salvation that God offers me requires of me an effort to work for the advancement of other men. In the same way, the promotion of culture and education is not the same as conversion to faith. There is an equilibrium, an order, a relationship between nature and grace.

Yet, however separate the transcendence of God and his initiative toward men and history, there is still in man a capacity for God, a "power of obedience" not only in his individuality but also in his social nature.[28] Chenu understands "power of obedience" in the same sense as St. Thomas Aquinas: "In every creature there exists a power of obedience insofar as every creature obeys God in order to receive in himself what God wishes of him." This power of obedience has to be seen in terms of history for one to perceive its relevance to the "signs of the times." In this way, for example, the dominion that man exercises over nature, or greater understanding of people, the culture of the spirit, the education of the heart, and so many other values, are "a power that obeys God in order to receive what God wishes."

All these human values, however, are equivocal; that is, they can remain on the temporal level or, worse, they can become (through pride) "idols" or they can be motives of hope ("powers of obedience"). For example, the process of socialization provides great resources for the practice of brotherly love; the declaration of human rights enunciates principles that are based on nature and define truth, justice, and love, which grace will guarantee in their active consistency in their own laws; world solidarity is an admirable basis and a sort of invitation for the catholicity of the Church; the advancement of new peoples is a call to the missionary task of the Church; brotherhood among men is an invitation to ecumenism without disputes. This means that all these human values exist in *hope* of the grace that will inform them from within, through conscience and the action of the sons of God. There is therefore a whole social dimension to the "power of obedience." Considered in this light, these human values are an "evangelical preparation." Faced with the signs of the times, we must "listen to them, discern them and interpret them in the light of the Holy Spirit: the people of God need to value them in the light of the divine Word so that revealed truth can be better perceived, better understood and expressed in more adequate forms."[29]

Let us now return to the object of our study. The author of *A Theology of Liberation* reminds us that the "signs of the times" are not only a call to intellectual analysis, "they are above all a call to pastoral activity, to commitment and to service." One cannot but agree with this call to pastoral activity; nevertheless, certain questions remain. If I have quoted and followed Chenu in this account of the "signs of the times," it is for two reasons: first, for the obvious authority he wields on the matter, and second, because he is one author, among others,[30] whom Gutiérrez presents as an authority. So it is worth examining what Gutiérrez says about the "signs of the times" in the light of Chenu's account.

The first thing that springs to light is that while Chenu attempts to describe and even define these signs, Gutiérrez makes no such attempt. How, then, can he present them as an important factor in the effort to produce a "new way of doing theology"? For Chenu, the signs of the times, precisely "as powers of obedience," respect the gratuity, transcendence, and distinction of the natural order and grace, whereas the contrary is suggested by Gutiérrez. This will become clear from a reading of his chapter 9, "Liberation and Salvation" (pp. 149–187). If it is true that the salvation brought by Christ includes the liberation brought about by history, it is also true—and here I differ from Gutiérrez—that the former is above the latter and saves it from the inherent possibility of loss through the exercise of human freedom. History alone cannot save us from this defectibility. History has only a "power of obedience" for salvation.

Chenu speaks of this "power of obedience" and states that he understands it in the same way as St. Thomas Aquinas. Now for Aquinas the power of obedience is not proportionately related in a direct way to the act and the effect that will stem from it. So Chenu, speaking of profane history and the history of salvation, of nature and grace, tells us that there is not a causal relationship between them. Historical progress and human advancement are not proportionate and therefore cannot of themselves bring about the life of God in the world. The power of obedience "obeys God": the creature in which this power is found is subject to obedience to God and the effect of grace will be proportionate to the action of the love of God, not to the natural dynamism of the creature or of history. This is why the signs of the times "hope for, announce and prepare"—but are not identified with—the kingdom. The signs of the times in the world "obey," are subject to, God, who in the economy of the Incarnation prolongs his action through the Church. The world waits for the Church; the world is not the Church.

A theology of the signs of the times[31] should not be confused with an opportunist counsel to adapt oneself to circumstances. Instead, it is a theology of obedience to the word of God, so that the sons of God can accept this word, let it work in them, and through their filial conscience decipher history. Men will be able to lead history, through obedience in charity, to its destiny, to the point to which God has called it through his word. This is a mystery of obedience to the love and initiative of the Father.

A theology of the signs of the times respects the primacy and transcendence of the Word and of revealed fact; it in no way means that this Word is removed from the history of the world, but, on the contrary, that it became flesh among men, although it remains distinct from what humanity can produce by itself. This theology, knowing that it finds its strength in the Word of God, directs pastoral activity and responds to the hope that creation—man and the world, with all its values—has with respect to God. A theology of the signs of the times, taking on these "powers of obedience," is very different from what Gutiérrez would suggest.

I do not see how a true understanding of these signs can become a factor of influence on a "new way of doing theology." Interpretation of the signs of the times in the light of the word supposes a knowledge of this word, and we have seen that Gutiérrez tends toward doctrinal impoverishment. Furthermore, he would interpret this same word through a political hermeneutics of the gospel.

A Particular Philosophy

No dismissiveness is implied in this heading, which would be to negate the value of the philosophy of action as preached by the great philosopher Maurice Blondel. I call it "particular" simply because Gutiérrez refers to a particular philosophy which appears to be another factor in the "new way of doing theology" which he is setting out for us.

Gutiérrez, who has no particular ax to grind with regard to the relationship between theology and any particular philosophy—or even with philosophy as a whole, since he claims that reason can be represented in its meeting with faith by the social sciences—is now concerned with one particular philosophy,

that of *action*. From the philosophical point of view, he prob-
ably sees a relationship between action and social praxis, or
"historical praxis," a concept he fails to define. In the end, it
would seem that action and praxis can come to mean much the
same thing. Referring to the philosophy of action, he quotes
Blondel, but without citing a particular page which would enable us to see the specific point of contact between Blondel's
thought and his own. He also mentions two works by Duméry
and recommends them to his readers as "a good treatment of
Blondelian methodology."[32]

Since we are urged to study Duméry in order to understand
Blondelian methodolgy, let us look at his works. Is Gutiérrez
aware that Duméry is opposed to interpreters of Blondel who
ignore or are unaware of the world of ideas and their representa-
tions and logical sequence, and not to the realities represented
in this way, since they can be apprehended only through action,
through living thought? Whether Duméry gives an accurate
interpretation of Blondel's thought is debatable—that is,
whether Blondel intended to make philosophy a purely reflective process of criticism.[33] But if we assume that he did, is this
a tenable point of view? Is it possible to dissociate idea from
being and make the latter the object of a thought process which
is not philosophy? This is what the debate is about: philosophy
would exercise itself on ideas, ideas of being, but without reaching the reality that these ideas represent. Is this conceivable?

First of all, the living consciousness on which reflective
thought is exercised is also thought, and this is what reaches
reality. How does it reach it, except perhaps through knowledge? If this is the case, how can one affirm that this knowledge
is a different type from that by which the ideas of these realities
are seized? If we are to be sincere, such a position calls the whole
business of the object of understanding into question: intelligible
connections, if not based on the necessity of being, would be
based on an *a priori* necessity of their own which cannot be
explained. Going back to meet being immediately through
choice is no way to overcome Kantianism, since heterogeneity,

accepted at the point of departure between the understandable universe of ideas and the real universe of being, makes the intellectual justification that is claimed for the choice chimerical. This option, this choice, is still an arbitary act, with no noetic value from the moment the knowledge that claims to justify it ceases to be knowledge of the being that it claims to reach. Blondel's philosophical undertaking fights against the impossibility, which it comes across so many times and never overcomes, of reaching being when one has not started from it.[34] But rather than spend more time on one interpreter of Blondel, even though he is the one whom Gutiérrez recommends to us, we should spend a moment or two on the philosophy of Blondel himself.

There are some aspects of Blondel's philosophy that concern our current theme. In view of the different interpretations of this thought, it is not easy to seize his thought without special application. Also, it is fair to ask whether Gutiérrez has made this application, since he does not give us a page reference in his efforts to present Blondel as a factor of influence in his new theological methodology.

From the great variety of interpretations of Blondel's thought, one can only conclude that his philosophical system often shows a lack of inner coherence. He devotes himself to the study of theological problems and tries to resolve them through philosophical means. This is where we come to the true source of the obscurities, confusions, and frequent backward steps with which his work abounds. This, too, is where Blondel compromises the gratuitousness of the supernatural order by using a philosophical method which tries to prove the necessity of the supernatural through purely rational analysis of human action. To say that he compromises the gratuitousness of the supernatural is not to say that he denies it, but that his thought fails to give a sufficient explanation of it.

Let us now return to Gutiérrez, who claims that Blondel "contributed to the elaboration of a new *apologetics* and became one of the most important thinkers of contemporary theology, including the most recent trends." In what way can Blondel be said to be an important theological thinker when it is precisely through his confusion between philosophy and theology that his apologetics comes into such serious difficulties? As J. H. Nicolas observed, "What is the value of a philosophy that requires faith, at least as a working hypothesis, and which sets out to verify this hypothesis as its aim?"[35] Yet it is precisely as a philosopher that Blondel claims to contribute to apologetics.

The other aspect of Blondel's thought is the difficulty he found, and did not always overcome, in freeing himself from subjectivism. When one does not start with being, it is impossible to reach it in the end. Indeed, Blondel's ideas have given rise to many controversies and opposing schools. If one sets out to criticize Blondel, one can find texts that say one thing and others that say the opposite. Can a philosophy that does not resolve the problem of how to reach and grasp its object through knowledge lay claim to absolute guarantee?

But there is another aspect that concerns Gutiérrez's work more directly: whether Blondel's view of the importance of action has the same meaning as Gutiérrez's. Blondel is speaking, above all, of the moral action of the human spirit, while Gutiérrez is speaking of action understood as "historical praxis." There is, therefore, a great difference between them. But even if we take action as basically moral action, it concerns only one part of philosophy, that is, moral philosophy. If all philosophy is to tend to a study of action, this would be an undue restriction of this science to one of its objects, that is, human destiny, without taking account of philosophy's deepest intentions, which are to be a speculative and contemplative science.

Now if we pass to action that is understood as "historical praxis," as Gutiérrez understands it, praxis cannot embrace the whole of being to which our understanding is orientated. This would have serious consequences in theology. If philosophy is a broader field than action, one can with greater reason say that theology, which is as broad as revelation and faith, goes far beyond the field of "praxis." For these reasons I cannot agree with Gutiérrez's judgment: "Another factor, this time of a *philosophical* nature, reinforces the importance of human action as the point of departure for all reflection." Rather, I would say that being is anterior to action and that the intuition and consideration of being are anterior to reflection upon action. These are the true objects of philosophy.[36] If this philosophical factor presents so many insoluble difficulties, I do not see how Gutiérrez can claim it as a proper basis for justifying his new theology.

The Confrontation with Marxist Thought

Gutiérrez's next factor is the influence of Marxist thought "focusing on praxis." This is the place for a broad general study of Marxist thought, which has often been made, both of Marxism in itself and Marxism as seen in the "theology of liberation" by its various protagonists, including Gustavo Gutiérrez.[37]

Since Gutiérrez talks in a very general way of the relationship between theology and Marxism, our commentary will be equally general. He tells us that "contemporary theology does in fact find itself in direct and fruitful confrontation with Marxism." What does he mean by "fruitful confrontation"? In what way can confrontation with Marxism be said to be "fruitful" for theology? "Confrontation" can mean various things, from a simple description of a relationship of place to a description of a form of affinity or mutual attraction between persons and things. Presumably, we are dealing here with a form of mutual attraction, and if this is the case we need to know something of Gutiérrez's sympathies with regard to Marxism. He quotes Sartre as saying: "Marxism as the formal framework of all contemporary philosophical thought cannot be superseded." Gutiérrez does not react against this statement in any way or indicate that he does not agree with it. Furthermore, he goes on to say: "It is to a large extent due to Marxist influence that theological thought, searching for its own sources, has begun to reflect on the meaning of the transformation of this world and the action of man in history."

His sympathy for Marxism is therefore evident. His "confrontation" is then a sort of comparison that is not devoid of admiration. We now have a situation where theology, "searching for its own sources," is going to be stimulated in its reflection on the "transformation of this world" by Marxism. Little by little, theology is going to learn from Marxism. Some confrontation! His next sentence makes his thought clearer: "Further, this confrontation helps theology to perceive what its efforts at understanding the faith receive from the historical praxis of man in history, as well as what its own reflection might mean for the transformation of the world." This means, in effect, that in order to carry out the "transformation of the world," theology receives and benefits from the efforts and experiences of Marxism.

Cardinal Koenig, speaking of atheism as a "dramatic attempt to extinguish the light of the living God," has said that "this fact of contemporary atheism was the spur of the Council."[38] Faced with this fact, the council made an express effort to guide our conscience as believers. It invited us to a confrontation in the spirit of dialogue and understanding, not in the attempt to pronounce judgment. This means making an effort to understand the reasoning and difficulties of atheism in order to understand its lack of understanding, with the object of enlightening it and helping it. This is not a matter of mere courtesy but a dialogue and a confrontation. In this dialogue there will always be something to receive from the other partner, since "the root of contestation is generally the way from primitive faith to reflective faith."[39]

This does not mean, however, that one has to listen without reacting. One has to try to respond, thanks to greater powers of reflection, with the same strength and the same loyalty. Dialogue has its spiritual requirements, and they do not consist in abdicating from reasoning; we must in no way renounce the use of our reason. Truth and the truth of faith are not possessions that we can shrug off in order to reach a "greater understanding" of the other. We have to take care to distinguish between what is ours—our tastes, affections, passions, prejudices, failings —and what belongs to the truth of God, given us through the word and through faith. We cannot dispense with them even if the situation appears to "require" it. An evaporation of faith cannot be called a purification of faith, and the betrayal of faith cannot be held to be a deepening of faith.

But there is more. In order to establish a fruitful dialogue with atheism—and the term applies to Marxism in this case—one has to be careful to reach a rigorous understanding of it. "When two schools of thought oppose each other, there is a natural tendency for each to spontaneously 'understand the other,' that is to engulf it. This is the natural strategy of contemporary atheism in its most specific aspect."[40] Contemporary atheism presents itself with the declaration that it does not wish to dispose of faith but to "develop" it, "purify" it, etc. Instead of attacking the mysteries head-on or denying that they contain truth, contemporary atheism tries to "explain" them in order to "understand" them. It therefore proposes a sort of hermeneutics of the Christian mysteries, telling us that they certainly have a true sense, in the understanding that faith and theology have had of them until now, but that they enshrine a "deeper meaning" that theology has not yet discovered and that the various brands of atheism can "interpret" for us in order to reach their "truer" meaning. This "truer" meaning, needless to say, will be a purely human meaning. In this way, for example, Marx, basing himself on Feuerbach, tells us that he set himself the task of realizing the human basis of Christianity in a secular way. This is the strategy of contemporary atheism which favors a general shift of thought: the question of "meaning," of "significance."

If the theologian and the Christian are not to be understood in the sense alluded to earlier, there is no option but to "understand" atheism and Marxism. He has to discern the elements of truth in them that he should take into his own thought. At the same time, he has to discern the elements of "error" or "illusion" that he might have allowed to infiltrate his thought, and reject them. He has to discern the limits of "true progress," reached in the understanding that mankind now has of itself. But he also has to detect what underlies the strategy of a "falsifying" hermeneutics, its "true" springs and its alleged lack of substance. He should not be afraid to show that such a hermeneutics, despite its "pretensions" to depth, often does no more than diminish an object that it allegedly fails to understand and often has not studied seriously.

Such observations should be taken into account in any dialogue with Marxism. Only thus can it be a "fruitful confrontation." However, I would question Gutiérrez's attitude to Marxism. Theologians who have studied his work have shown how he sacrifices essential elements of our faith in his dialogue with Marxism. It is not that he denies them but that he reduces the content of his faith. If this is so, one would have to say that instead of Marxism's being a factor that influences the "new approach" to theology, this "new approach" will be a service to Marxism, which is already widespread in Latin America. Instead of "understanding" Marxism, theology will be "understood" by it. Marxism will have convinced Gutiérrez of the need for a Marxist rereading of the gospel and of the Bible in general.

Eschatology and Historical Praxis

Gutiérrez's next page (p. 10) deals with subjects that are both difficult and important: eschatology, history, orthodoxy, orthopraxis, and historical praxis. Together, they constitute another factor that influences the "new approach" to theology.

First, let us look at a statement which the author does not bother either to justify or to explain more fully: "If human history is, above all else, an opening to the future, then it is a task, a political occupation." He assumes that history is, above all else, "an opening to the future." Does this statement not need some sort of qualification?

The theological problem of history is difficult and much has been written on the subject.[41] Also, from a philosophical point of view, it is important to distinguish the various meanings that the concept of a history, orientated toward the future, can have. If one admits a futurist dimension in history, one can fall into absurdity, as did Sartre in speaking of the free man—he could not admit there is a way ahead for him which had not been traced in advance: "I am condemned to have no law other than my own."[42]

We can agree that man makes history, works out his destiny, and has an inalienable responsibility for it. His freedom and his actions can transform the realities of this world for better or for worse, and he can certainly impress a new meaning on things and on his contacts with his fellow men; but man continues to be dependent on a destiny that God, in his wisdom and love, has freely set for him. History unfolds toward a future that man works out in freedom, though not without certain deep laws which have been impressed both on the realities with which man works and on his own conscience and freedom which impel him to work. In this way history also depends on a past, not only through external historical conditionings but through a law which antedates all human existence and which might be called "the priority of nature." But if, on the contrary, we take account of the fact that philosophy has done an almost complete about-turn in the direction of man himself, divorced from the concept of human nature, we will find it very difficult to understand what man is. Is he a mental structure or a focus of consciousness, or of freedom or a history or a moment of a history? Whatever he is, he no longer has a human nature; in particular, he no longer is a human who is capable of formulating bases for a morality of individual action and of dictating its ends and values to the human person.

Coming back to Gutiérrez, we find that he is further preparing the ground for his new concept of theology. This extremely succinct announcement of his concept of history and of eschatology hides serious and indeed insuperable difficulties, from the point of view of both philosophy and theology.

From the point of view of philosophy, we are entitled to ask

what criteria he would use for openness to the future, what laws
will regulate his task of building the world, and what criteria
will direct his political occupation. If history and man himself
are defined as "future," with no further definition, I do not see
what answer he can give to these questions, since there is no law
or motive that governs man's task in any particular instance.
But, of course, if one gives "historical praxis" the central place
in a philosophy of history, the problems are meaningless. Why?
Let us listen to Karl Marx:

> The question of knowing whether human thought pos-
> sesses an objective truth is not a theoretical question but
> a practical one. It is in practice that man must prove the
> truth—that is the reality and vigour, the realistic charac-
> ter—of his thought. The controversy over the reality or
> nonreality of a thought separated from practice is a purely
> scholastic question.[43]

For many Marxists, praxis is not only a criterion of truth but
the basis of the whole process of knowledge, from beginning to
end. We know that for "philosophical Soviet" Marxism, praxis
is the material activity of man and all theoretical and spiritual
activity is explicitly excluded from it. The category of "material
activity" means, above all, the production of material goods, but
also the class struggle, political life, and even the part played by
the physical and material perfectioning of scientific and artistic
activity. This praxis serves to establish the criterion of truth,
insofar as truths are verified in praxis—"verified" not only in the
sense of "brought about" but in the sense of "actually making
true."

What does Gustavo Gutiérrez think of all this? He certainly
gives us some pointers. In the first place, historical praxis occupies a central place: "The rediscovery of the *eschatological dimension* in theology has led us to consider the central role of
historical praxis." Clearly, we would see history, or more precisely man in history, as essentially political—understanding

this term as broader than the question of power groups. But man is not exhausted in his political activities; he has others, which go beyond the political field. Yet the general tenor of Gutiérrez's work does not seem to indicate that he shares this view. For him, the political occupation is so important that "the future of the Church depends on the number and the strength of the Christians who recognize the need for the struggle and join the files of the world proletariat."⁴⁴ This is surely enough to show the importance he gives to "historical praxis," to the class struggle and political occupation—the "transformation" of this world. What more is needed to show that Gustavo Gutiérrez understands historical praxis in a Marxist sense?

We saw at the outset how often Gutiérrez talks of praxis and that, although the term is so relevent to his work, he fails to define it. There is not even a precise definition of the sense in which he understands the term. However, as we go through the book the elements that make it up and determine the sense in which it is used gradually come to the fore. Its meaning is virtually the same as that assigned to it by Marxist terminology. In effect, "praxis" for Marxism, as we have seen, is formed of "the material activity of man."

Routkevitch defined the term this way in a discussion with other Soviet leaders, and his point was the exclusion of theoretical and spiritual activity from its definition. The main components of material activity are the production of material goods, the class struggle, political life, and the side of scientific and artistic achievement that brings about bodily and material advancement. The political dimension of the gospel is presented as a principle of hermeneutics for the class struggle, for the drastic reduction of the life of the Church—at least in some texts—to political praxis, to a praxis which itself becomes the criterion of truth: "Only by doing this truth will our faith be 'verified.' " All of this enables us to see the Marxist character of Gutiérrez's conception of praxis. Thus one can say that, from the philosophical point of view, his vision of history suffers from the difficulties that are inherent in the Marxist concept of history.

Turning to the theological aspect, we must examine the results of a union between the theological concept of eschatology and the unpurified Marxist concept of historical praxis. I would agree that one of the most important contributions of present-day theology is the revaluation of the eschatological dimension of our Christian life. Above all, to speak of the eschatological dimension is to speak in theological terms of the "time of the Church."[45] This "time of the Church" means the time that elapses between the two comings of Christ, during which salvation is at once brought about and, in the course of being brought about, sees the Church on its way to its definitive meeting with the Lord. It is also seen as God's saving eschatological community, because the promised Messiah has been manifest in Jesus of Nazareth, has been elevated by God to his right hand, and has sent the Church the Holy Spirit. The authors of the New Testament, open to the eschatological future, do not fail, however, to give sufficient emphasis to what has already been brought about (2 Cor 5:17, Heb 4). But this eschatological time is not to be spent merely in looking backward and forward. Already, the early Christian community was conscious of the joy experienced in primitive Christian worship (Acts 2:46, 1:6), in access to the sacrament of baptism, in which salvation was experienced (1 Pt 1:6, 8). Christian existence always stretches between the two poles of grace, that which is already won in Christ and that which is still to come. Christian existence lives on the basis of grace already received and salvation that is hoped for without fear, but it calls into play all the virtues of the Christian, on his way, with the Church, toward the definitive coming of the kingdom.

A true rediscovery of eschatology has to bring out the elements that constitute this "time of the Church." Eschatology is centered on Christ, and man lives this era of grace and love to the extent that he unites himself to Christ through his faith and through the sacraments, truly *in mysterio,* but secretly waiting for the manifestation of the glory of Christ and of his own glory on the last day. The key to the explanation and the realization of eschatology is Christ, the sacrament of the Trinity; Christ is the primordial sacrament.[46]

Through the Incarnation the Word became man. Like every human person, he showed himself to other men in a sensible way, occupying his place in history and in the community of men, making himself fundamentally present to the men of his generation through the sole fact of being present to all of them in a virtual way. But in knowing and loving this man, in entering into contact with him, men were knowing, loving, and entering into contact with the divine person of the Word, because this man was the Word. He was known, loved, and adored as such, as this divine Person, through faith. Jesus not only led to knowledge of the Word but was the Word. Because of this, the experience in faith that the apostles had of Christ was an eschatological experience, because there can be no more perfect knowledge than what is given in Christ. Now the Church's confession of faith reenacts the eschatological experience of the apostles. This reenactment of the experience of the apostles allows the Church to eject all sophist criteria of every epoch and every culture, however up to date they may be. As Le Guillou has written: "In the Paschal confession of Christ (1 Tm 6:13) we are given access to knowledge of the Father, the eschatological norm of the apostolic witness." In this way the apostolic confession of faith, since it *eschatologically* marks the Paschal Passover from the old world to the new, cannot be reduced to a simple historical fact that each new generation can interpret as it likes. This apostolic confession has a normative quality which is not at the mercy of a historical mentality, because it derives from the mystery of the Trinity, which is permanently at work in the Church. The Holy Spirit provides the Church with an "eschatological memory" and maintains the actuality of its faith (Rom 8:6).

This radical aspect of eschatology is very often overlooked. Eschatological meaning is restricted to the future—and what a future! Often this means the transformation of the world, as understood in the sense of material transformation, or at least it fails to underline sufficiently the genuine *eschatological* character, which must mean a reenactment in us, through faith, of a meeting with Christ, the divine Person, and manifestation of the mystery of the Trinity.

This, as theology has traditionally noted, underlines the importance for the Church of the keynote of apostolicity, which unfailingly expresses the continuity between the Church of today and of all times with the Church of the apostles, thanks to the apostolic succession. But there is something further: the Church, as the sacrament of the mystical body, refers us to a saving present that is contained within the Church. The Church is both sign and cause of salvation because it is the sign of what God is doing now to save those who accept salvation. It is the sign of the salvation which is being brought about. Since Christ saves through the mystery of his cross and Resurrection, the Church is in this sense the sacrament of the Paschal mystery.

Finally, the Church, as the sacrament of Christ, refers us to a future it already, in a certain way, contains. It refers us to Christ, who "is to come"; it announces his glorious second coming and the fulfillment of redemption. This, another aspect of the eschatological dimension, means that the Church is not of this world (Jn 17:14), even when it has to be "in the world" (Jn 17:11). This is one of the higher principles that should illuminate these very difficult problems of the relationship between the Church and the world. It should not be forgotten that the Church is eschatological. By this I do not mean that this principle alone is enough to resolve all these problems, but it should never be forgotten that this celestial Church is the end to which the earthly Church tends. It tends toward this heavenly Church with all its being and all its dynamism, and this is how the kingdom of God is brought about. It is impossible to understand the Church on earth if one abstracts from its internal ordination and its definitive fulfillment in the Church of heaven.

However, let us come back to the author we are analyzing. If one compares the foregoing considerations from a theological viewpoint with what our author offers us, one sees a reduction

and disfigurement of what theology understands as eschatological. So if the rediscovery of the "eschatological" dimension is
another factor in his "new approach to theology," he is dealing
with a mutilated and disfigured eschatology in the service of his
new project. Let us look at the problem a little more closely.

I have said that Gutiérrez *reduces* the riches of the eschatological dimension. In effect, he fails to make us see, and fails to
bear in mind, that "eschatological" has to be understood principally in relation to the mystery of the Word made flesh; that a
living eschatology means to live dependent on the great happen-
ing of the past, made present in the Church through the sacraments, the word, the life of the Church, and to live in hope of
a future, with the whole weight of responsibility that this implies. Gutiérrez, on the other hand, speaks only of openness to
the future. Hence his silence on major factors which are indispensable for a true understanding of eschatology. Where in his
thought is the apostolic succession, the magisterium of the
Church, the transmission of a word received from the Father in
Christ, which cannot be reduced to any system?[47]

The New Testament suggests a theological understanding of
the "time" of history. Openness to the future means openness
to "him who is to come," and this is why the Church both
experiences and announces that the Risen One is near and that
everyone, together with the Church, should remain open "to the
moment" *(kairos)* that is fixed by God for the glorious manifestation of his Son. It is therefore not just a matter of wandering
aimlessly toward the future. Above all—and here is a disfigurement of eschatology—"openness to the future" does not mean
precisely the same thing as "political occupation," although it
includes it. Much less are these phrases synonymous when
"political occupation" and "historical praxis," with their subtle
Marxist echoes, are elevated into a criterion of truth.

The author tells us that "our faith will be 'verified' " only by
"doing this truth," by which he refers to the "building up of that
brotherhood and communion in history." There are two very
distinct things here. One is that the response of faith to the Lord

should include the attempt to transform the world, in the sense of temporal betterment under all its aspects, but should lead beyond that—to the meeting with the Lord in faith, hope, and love. The other is that the object of our faith is "verified," that is, becomes true in itself, only to the extent that it contributes to the transformation of the world. The distinction is particularly important if we bear in mind the latent Marxist thought which holds the criterion of *verification* to be above that of absolute truth, such as the following, proposed by Routkevitch.

> All the basic theses and a great quantity of particular Marxist-Leninist theses of philosophy, economics, the theory of socialism and the class struggle are absolutely true. That matter is the first element and consciousness the derived element, that the ruin of capitalism is inevitable, that the socialist order will take over from capitalism as inevitably as day follows night, that the socialist economic system opens unlimited space to the development of productive forces, etc., are *absolute truths* proved in practice to the extent that nothing in the future can call them into question.[48]

On the other hand, how can all the experiences of faith that are possible to man possibly be *verified,* that is, proved, made true, and whose are the criteria for the sign that this has been done? This *verification* must exclude the hidden inner life of many Christians. Therefore it should not surprise us that, in practice, many theologians and adherents of this "new theology" are unwilling to waste their time in works and tasks that are nonpolitical, not concerned with the class struggle, since such works and tasks cannot serve to *verify* faith and the coming of the kingdom. For example, it is a fact that in the two Latin American countries in which this theology has taken deepest root, attention to the contemplative life has declined. The reason for this is that, in accord with "historical praxis" as a criterion of truth, the coming of the kingdom cannot be *verified* in monasteries.

To follow this criterion of "verification" would surely be to the profound detriment of men and the world. As Congar has noted, the hope and salvation that the Church has to announce and preach to the world is also, and principally, a salvation from that from which the world cannot be saved by itself, and even, perhaps, from that from which the world does not want to be saved, or is ignorant that it has to be saved. The world does not know that it has to be saved from deeper and more secret alienations than the political or sociological.[49]

Conclusions on Gutiérrez's Section on Historical Praxis

The section titled "Historical Praxis" is devoted to an enumeration of eight factors that Gutiérrez considers justify his "new approach to theology," rather than to an open definition of what he understands by the phrase. These factors are the following:

1. The biblical vision of faith and charity
2. The evolution of spirituality
3. Anthropological aspects of revelation
4. The very life of the Church
5. The signs of the times
6. The philosophy of action
7. The influence of Marxist thought
8. Eschatology and historical praxis

The mere listing of these themes shows the richness of the theology of the Church, but it is a pity that Gutiérrez deals with them so briefly and distorts them to his own purpose. Such a richness of themes occupies hardly more than four pages. What is worse is that he puts the themes forward as creative factors in a "new theology" in a sense very different from what they should have. It fills me with sorrow and indignation to see the mysteries that the Lord has entrusted to the reflection of our faith treated in this way.

We now have to prepare ourselves for the triumphal arrival

of the "new way of doing theology." Gutiérrez considers that he is able to present us with a promising theology since he has tried, through the art of simplification and defamation, to ruin the wisdom and scientific functions of theology. I have already alluded to this, in speaking of the "evaporation" of these functions, which, thus evaporated, the author has the cheek to tell us "are essential and permanent." He is also emboldened to proceed by his enumeration of these eight factors—all great themes of theology—which he sees as contributing to his project but which we have seen as failing to justify the "new approach" that he suggests to the theological task.

Chapter 5
Theology as "Critical Reflection"

Having enumerated the factors that led him to his concept of theology, Gutiérrez gives what he claims are the results, embodied in two general conclusions. The first is: "All the factors we have considered have been responsible for a more accurate understanding that communion with the Lord inescapably means a Christian life centred around a concrete and creative commitment of service to others." The second is: "They have likewise led to the rediscovery or explicit formulation of the function of theology as critical reflection. It will be well at this point to define further our terms."

We have already said something about the first conclusion in the section on charity as the center of the Christian life. Communion with the Lord implies and requires love of one's neighbor—loving him because of our very love of God. Charity is a true friendship with God; the good that lies at the heart of this friendship is the very good of God, which has become the good of the spiritual creature through grace. Now this communication of grace is made, or at least offered, to all spiritual creatures. In this way, he who has charity will find himself a friend, in the deepest sense of the word, of all spiritual creatures since he communes with them in the same and identical destiny, consisting in reaching happiness in God.

In this sense, I am completely in agreement with Gutiérrez insofar as loving God *implies* loving one's neighbor. "If someone says he loves God and does not love his brother he is a liar," Scripture tells us. I also agree that this charity toward one's neighbor takes on a social and political dimension and that we

77

have to commit ourselves to specific service to others. But here one must add that Christian charity toward one's neighbor is specific to Christianity. It is not a matter of loving one's neighbor for *whatever* reason but *because* of the Lord.

Our response to the love of God demands our dedication and service to our neighbor as part of the very love that we have for the Lord. But loving means wanting and procuring the good of the loved one, and what is specific to Christianity is that in loving our neighbor we seek above all—though not only—to bring about his calling, his call toward God. To invert the order of the goods we procure for our neighbor—that is, to seek first, above all or exclusively, his temporal good—is not charity. It may be love, but it is not the love of Christ. In this sense, though perhaps impelled by the pressing and widespread poverty and injustice in Latin America, Gutiérrez does not bring out the importance and the primacy of the good of God, which we should try to procure for our neighbor in the exercise of love.

But where I part company totally with him, as I have said, is in his claim that "communion with the Lord inescapably means the Christian life centred around concrete and creative commitment of service to others." Loving God—communion with the Lord—means much more than commitment to our neighbor. Love of God takes priority over love of our neighbor, not only because it is God who asks us to love our neighbor but because the love of God extends beyond the sphere of our relationships with our neighbor. To think otherwise would be to forget the transcendence of God and to forget that man lives in strict dependence on him. It would be to forget that we are called to an intimacy that is based on a communion of thought and will, which constitutes the center of the happiness of God. The Father seeks to be adored "in spirit and in truth." If it were otherwise, the Christian religion would only run the risk of sinning against its neighbor, whereas, on the contrary, we are fully aware of the depth of evil and malice into which man can fall.

Let us now concentrate on the second conclusion, which

refers to the critical function of theology that Gutiérrez, sets out to define. One after the other, he shows us the forms of theology as "critical reflection." In the first place, theology has to be critical of itself and its basic principles and, therefore, has to be in full possession of its conceptual instruments. But before one asks what the author understands as criticizing the basic principles of theology, one can remind him that he has failed to be critical in what he has put before us. He has not been critical of the concept of "historical praxis." He has not been critical of Marxism, whose "scientific" character he takes as an established fact. Indeed, a number of serious studies on Marxism show its inconsistencies in the economic, social, anthropological, religious, and philosophical fields.[1] Gutiérrez, however, does not adopt a critical attitude to the Marxist system; and his failure to criticize it is even more serious in a theologian because declarations by John XXIII and Paul VI recommend a critical attitude, even rejection, of Marxist ideas which are "against the nature of man and opposed to the Christian concept of life."[2] What, then, does he mean by saying that theology should be critical of itself and its basic principles?

If we are to debate the author on this point, we need a common understanding of theology, at least in its essential points. We might agree with the expression "theology stems from the encounter between faith and human reason." But I think we will disagree when we examine what this expression means for Gutiérrez, or for ourselves. But even if we can agree this far, what does he mean by saying that theology should criticize its basic principles? If we look at theology as it is, we see that it has a very specific character. Theology deals with a multitude of problems that have not stemmed solely from reasoned reflection on experience. These problems have reached the sphere of human reason only through revelation and they exist only for him who receives this revelation as coming from God. That is, they exist only for the believer. I am not saying that the truths of revelation exist only if man believes them but that these truths are a problem for reason only when man accepts them in faith. For example, the mystery of the Trinity is not an object of critical reflection for a nonbeliever.

This collection of truths on which human reason reflects has stemmed from a revelation from God, and man has begun by *accepting* the very fact of revelation, in faith. The act of faith by which this fact is accepted depends essentially on a voluntary choice. Of course the transcendent fact of revelation is accompanied by perceptible signs which make it reasonable to believe it, but the fact of revelation as such, in itself, is not verifiable. Even if it is certain that belief is reasonable, it is also certain that unbelief is not irrational.

From this it follows that the whole theological task and therefore all the conclusions to which it leads are intrinsically dependent on a preceding choice which does not stem from reason alone and cannot be imposed on reason as something necessary. For the person who makes this choice, theology does not exist as a form of knowledge. Theology is devoted to the very mysteries which are held to be true, and from this basis it tries to delve into truth and meaning. These objects of theology are beyond the competence of any philosophical or scientific discipline. Christian theology unfolds in the light of faith. Of course, it makes use of human reason under different titles, but its basic content has to be referred back to faith, one way or another. This, however, should not be taken as meaning that theology transcends reason to the extent that its truths, coming from divine revelation and accepted in faith, cannot enter into the sphere of human reason. This is the point at which human reason, illuminated by faith, seeks a greater understanding of the mysteries of God. Theology has sprung from faith and is supported in all its work by faith, but it is human reason that produces the discourses of theology. Theology depends on faith but it is not the faith.

Theology reflects on the truths of revelation that are accepted by faith, but revelation is a historical fact—and certainly a transcendent one in that it reaches believers of all periods; but since revelation is historical, it has been verified in successive epochs and has used human language, the fruit and expression of particular forms of culture. If one bears this in mind, one will see that the first preoccupation of theology should be to determine what God has revealed to man. This is the positive function of theology. Theological reflection on the content of revelation requires a positive study of the way in which God has made us experience, through his saving action, his divine being and the meaning of our human being. As a science of the content of revelation, theology should therefore look attentively to the Old and New Testaments and the writings of those doctors of the Church who have tried to recognize and understand the content of revelation throughout the course of history. It will likewise take account of the evolution of dogma.

However, it is not as a historian but formally as a theologian that the latter should approach this positive task. He may have recourse to the scientific methods of history, but positive theology is not a simple historical science. It is theology, and this has a terribly important meaning. It means that theology studies the sources of revelation and the witnesses of faith through the centuries, starting from the actual faith of the Church and under the guidance of the magisterium of the Church. Its studies use scientific historical method, but they are guided by faith and the direction of the magisterium. Using historical method this way, the theologian can decide in a "scientific" and therefore fallible manner—in a manner therefore subject to the supreme judgment of the magisterium—if a particular proposition has been effectively revealed, how it has been "lived" in the Church, and whether it is an authentic teaching of the Church.

The positive function of theology must be bathed in and inspired by the proper light of theology itself. The positive function cannot be anterior to theology; it *is* theology and therefore shares the light of theology, that is, reason that is in constant touch with faith and is therefore constantly referred to the magisterium.

Taking account of all this, we are now in a position to see what is meant by the statement that theology should be critical of itself and its basic principles. Theology, as we have seen, cannot be above faith. Theology is made of faith. The theological reasoning cannot criticize its own object in the sense of opposing or modifying it. It understands it in the light of faith and sees how it becomes true.

We have seen that positive theology uses historical method; likewise, the speculative function of theology uses philosophy and other sciences, such as psychology. Although history, philosophy, and psychology are autonomous sciences, when they are used as instruments of theology they are used to scrutinize mysteries or truths—principles of life that are beyond the natural objects of these other sciences. Thus theology, in using these sciences in its theological task, rather than depending on them, judges them its instruments. In this way theology exercises a critical function on these sciences. It cannot depend on them, because it depends on the word, received through faith, in believing reason.

What does Gutiérrez think of this critical function? He says only that theology must be critical of itself and its basic principles. He gives no explanation of what he might mean, with all the consequences that his silence on this point brings. Faith, in fact—or if one prefers, the articles of faith are the bases or principles of theology. How, then, can theology prove or criticize these articles of faith?

Next, Gutiérrez tells us that theology must also take "a clear and critical attitude regarding economic and socio-cultural issues in the life and reflection of the Christian community." This is an urgent aspect of theology, particularly when one bears the Latin American situation in mind. I agree completely with Gutiérrez, that theology can use its own light to criticize everything that prevents men from reaching their authentic goal. These obstacles include—although they are not the only ones—economic and sociocultural conditions. There is no doubt that Gutiérrez's statements on this aspect, in this book and in his many articles and lectures, have been an enormous help in bringing the Church to an awakened consciousness of the conditions of poverty in this continent. This aspect of theology has gained enormously in importance in Latin America, thanks to the influence of Gustavo Gutiérrez.

On this point of criticism of economic and sociocultural conditioning, however, I would like to make two points. The first is that one of the essential ideas of Medellín, the "theology of the image," could be extended to cover criticism not only of these conditionings but also of others, such as those that stem from defective philosophical concepts that detract from a true conception of man. In this way we could correct the presentations that degrade man and could give him back his true identity, made in the image of God "in Christ Jesus." It is important to note the degradation of the image, through sin, in all its breadth and depth. It would be a liberating theology indeed that criticizes false novelties and tries to free man from them, putting in their place the "irreducible novelty of Christ." The logic of this critical function of theology should also be applied to the conditionings that stem from the Marxist system, as well as from the capitalist system and other ideologies. The fashionable currents of thought at the moment—Marxism, structuralism, Freudianism—tend to impose an image of "modern man" which is irreconcilable with the image of God which man bears in the depths of his being and which the Church should seek to discover. It is very easy to use these ideologies and to analyze man exclusively in the light of secular sciences, which, turned on the problem of faith, produce decisive changes in faith and sometimes lead to its total liquidation. Would it not be a great liberating benefit to give a true philosophy back to man?

The second observation on the critical aspect of theology is expression of a well-founded fear. Speaking of theology as "rational knowledge," Gutiérrez was far too vague in his definition of this "classic function of theology"; he was not nearly severe enough in his requirements, asking for no particular philosophy, not even the indispensable services of philosophy itself. He thought that philosophy could be substituted by psychology or sociology, and this is my great fear. How can one criticize the extravagances of sociology, psychology, or economics without an authentic philosophy, and how can the "good news" be made credible to modern man, in its possibility of realization, without making the whole of its riches clear, without knowledge of the depths and aspirations of man? The importance of economic and sociocultural conditionings can be considered objectively only when one knows what one means by man. The identity of man is revealed in the gospels, but how is unbelieving man to discover it? Hence the need for *a* philosophy, not just *any* philosophy, and without excluding the new discoveries of psychology, sociology, etc., in a perfect integration within this authentic philosophy.

Having considered these two aspects in which the critical function of theology appears—that is, criticism of its own basic principles and conceptual instruments and of the economic and sociocultural issues—Gutiérrez defines the most important aspect of critical reflection:

> But above all, we intend this term to express the theory of a definite practice. Theological reflection would then necessarily be a criticism of society and the Church insofar as they are called and addressed by the Word of God; it would be a critical theory worked out in the Light of the Word, accepted in faith and inspired by a practical purpose—and therefore indissolubly linked to historical praxis.

This statement is central to Gutiérrez's work since it is his attempt at defining his conception of theology and the reason for his enumeration of the different factors that brought him to this "new approach" to the theological task. This central text is completed and explained by the following, which I propose to quote at length and then to analyze.

> By preaching the Gospel message, by its sacraments and by the charity of its members, the Church proclaims and

shelters the gift of the kingdom of God in the heart of human history. The Christian community professes a "faith which works through charity." It is—at least ought to be—real charity, action and commitment to the service of men. Theology is reflection, a critical attitude. Theology *follows;* it is the second step. . . .

The pastoral activity of the Church does not flow as a conclusion from theological premises. Theology does not produce pastoral activity; rather it reflects upon it. . . .

A privileged *locus theologicus* for understanding the faith will be the life, preaching and historical commitment of the Church.

These central texts in the work of Gustavo Gutiérrez can only make us wonder again at the superficiality, contradictions, and sophisms that he tries to force upon us. It is superficial—given that this is an attempt at defining his promised theology—to offer us a definition of it in this way. We remember that he spoke of the "classic functions" of theology and, having stripped them to such an extent, still demanded that they should be permanent. He is now telling us that those functions will be subject to a "redefinition," under the criterion of the critical function he puts before us.

Perhaps one can say that this first chapter is not the whole book—agreed. But this first chapter is devoted to the idea of theology, and all that comes after is based on this concept of theology. It is superficial because he skates over themes that deserve much deeper attention, without pausing to measure the effect of his words. Such themes are "the object of theology," "the life of the Church as a *locus theologicus,*" "the relationship between theology and pastoral practice," and, again, "historical praxis." He will end with the political hermeneutics of the gospel, having made a brief allusion to the much debated historical period of the "new theology." One looks in vain for anything truly consistent in all these themes; nor does he lack contradictions. Compare these two quotes:

Theology does not produce pastoral activity, rather it re-flects upon it.

On the other hand, theology by pointing to the sources of revelation helps to orient pastoral activity; it puts it in a wider context.

I would agree that theology does not produce pastoral activ-ity, at least formally or necessarily, since pastoral activity springs from charity and apostolic zeal. But here we are talking of principles of pastoral theology insofar as this can be discussed "scientifically." If it could, there would not be so many "pasto-ral institutes" or conferences on the subject. Therefore, if we are talking in the same sense, the contradiction is unavoidable. Earlier he told us: "Theological reflection . . . would be a critical theory worked out in the light of the Word, accepted in faith and inspired by a practical purpose—and therefore indissolubly linked to historical praxis." Such a concept of theology, under-stood in the strict sense of the words, would have no great novelty, compared to what the great Scholastic doctors, St. Thomas, St. Albert, and St. Bonaventure, said on the subject. No great novelty, that is, except for two things: that for these three men the principal function of theology was not its critical function and that their way of being united to practice and "historical praxis" was very different. But for judging "in the light of the Word . . . and inspired by a practical purpose," it was the same. What else is St. Thomas saying in introducing the first and second parts of his section on morals: *"moralis enim circa agibilia versatur"*? What else is seen as *agibilia,* except the action through which man, in relation with God and with all men and the whole of creation, either journeys toward or away from his ultimate end? Can there be a more complete praxis?

Our author's contradiction lies in the fact that elsewhere he defined theology as an understanding of faith, but by "faith" he understands not the truth of the message but action, and action within very narrow limits: "In this light the understanding of the faith appears as the understanding not of the simple affirmation—almost memorization—of truths but of a commitment, an overall attitude, a particular posture toward life"; and elsewhere: "It [faith] is . . . real charity, action and commitment to the service of men. Theology is reflection, a critical attitude. Theology *follows;* it is the second step."

Perhaps Gutiérrez would say that these statements are not contradictory and in no way opposed to each other, and in fact he speaks elsewhere of seeking a balance, claiming that his "intention, however, is not to deny the meaning of *orthodoxy* understood as a proclamation of and reflection on statements considered to be true. Rather the goal is to balance and even to reject the primacy and almost exclusiveness which doctrine has enjoyed in Christian life." But we must note a very symptomatic fact: in none of the pages in which he describes the nature of theology does Gutiérrez affirm the primacy of revealed fact. Whenever he considers a doctrinal aspect of faith or theology, his reticence comes to the fore and he uses the somewhat obscure form of merely asking questions, as we have seen. Nevertheless, the importance he gives to praxis, because it is the "critical" function of theology that "redefines" the wisdom and rational functions, and the stress he lays on the political hermeneutics of the gospel—all this shows that, for him, theology is not theology of revelation but an understanding of "praxis," which is never defined. It is praxis that carries the primacy, and whatever he may say, he can never escape from this contradiction.

Finally, let me say that what he is setting out is not theology. The only sense in which he can keep his "theology" as a true theology is through an equivocal use of the *words* "understanding of faith." But it is not necessary for everything that is said to be understandable. The absurd can be pronounced, but it is not intelligible. This is where the *sophism* comes in. "The understanding of faith" does not mean "understanding of the accepted word" but "understanding in commitment." In speaking of theology as the understanding of faith, the author can make us think that this is a true theology, but the words, as he uses them, have another principal meaning. For him, the understanding of faith means the understanding of commitment.

If we bear all this in mind, we will see that there is an essential contradiction when he tells us that theology "would be a critical theory worked out in the light of the Word, accepted in faith."

Some years ago Jean Guitton expressed this view, which Congar has since said parallels his own:

> There are only two methods to bring about an alliance between tradition and the present, between the old and the new, between truth and conscience. The first consists in *first* and *particularly* defining tradition (which in the final analysis is the history of identity of truth) in order to possess it and understand it both in its formulas and in its spirit, or more exactly in the spirit of its formulas. *Then* trying to turn one's gaze on the thought of the world in which one lives and which we call the present-day world, knowing it in all its aspects in its letter and its spirit; *finally* this method consists in discerning what in this modern thought is in conformity with and what is in contradiction to the spirit of tradition, assimilating the first element which is substantial and rejecting the second which is corrupted.
>
> The second method consists in *first* and *above all* defining modern-day thought, taking its language, nourishing oneself on its principles and impregnating oneself with its spirit and *then* turning back to tradition, finally rejecting everything in this that appears contrary to modern thought and adapting everything else to modern thought.
> . . .
> The first method gives us either a confirmation of tradition and its expression and therefore a new understanding of its riches, or an unaccustomed expression which adds precision to traditional expression. . . . The second method gives us an expression of tradition in which this is recognizable to itself because if the expression is new its novelty consists in an alteration and not a definition. The first

method is that of those who could be called orthodox reformers . . . the second is that of heterodox reformers who can with greater justification be called innovators.[3]

Congar basically shares this account of the two methods, and I would do the same. So we can ask Gutiérrez this question: Which of these two methods is used by the *Theology of Liberation?* He cannot tell us that it is a mixture of the two since these two methods are basically in mutual opposition. They are opposed because one gives the primacy to the word and tradition and the other to "modern thought," of which there is no generally accepted definition. Neither can he tell us that it is neither one nor the other but something different. From the moment he tries to explain the union between faith and praxis, he has to give one or the other the primacy, not something else. Gutiérrez himself has said as much: "Theology thus understood, that is to say as linked to praxis, fills a prophetic function insofar as it interprets historical events with the intention of revealing and proclaiming their profound meaning." Now then, in this theology—which is linked to "praxis," which has the first place, the word of God as lived in tradition, that is, "praxis"—tradition cannot be the same thing as praxis.

What we are questioning here is which comes first, the word as lived in tradition or praxis; but there are two ways in which "coming first" can be understood. First, there is the primacy of what theology considers; that is, does it seek a greater understanding of God in his word or, on the other hand, of the events of praxis? The second question with regard to this primacy is this: By what criterion—in the light of what—is this critical judgment of theology established? Does one judge in the light of the word, accepted in faith, or does judgment stem from historical praxis?

Let us turn to the first aspect of the primacy that we seek to see established in theology. What is the object of theological study? Let us see what Gutiérrez has to say on the subject.

> But above all we intend this term to express the theory of
> a definite practice. Theological reflection would then nec-
> essarily be a criticism of society and the Church insofar as
> they are called and addressed by the Word of God.
> . . .
>   Theology is reflection, a critical attitude. Theology *fol-
> lows,* it is the second step. . . .
>   The intention is to recognise the work and importance
> of concrete behaviour, of deeds, of action, of praxis in the
> Christian life. . . .
>   In the last analysis this concern for praxis seeks to avoid
> the practices which gave rise to Bernanos' sarcastic re-
> mark: "God does not choose the same men to keep his
> Word as to fulfil it." . . .
>   The pastoral activity of the Church does not flow as a
> conclusion from theological premises. Theology does not
> produce pastoral activity; rather it reflects upon it. . . .
>   As critical reflection on society and the Church theolo-
> gy is an understanding which both grows and in a certain
> sense changes.

The last paragraph sounds like something that could resemble
the progress of the Church in the understanding of faith, but let
us not be deceived. We are not dealing here with progress in the
understanding of faith but with growth, with change in criticism
of society and the Church. In these texts the term "praxis"
comes to occupy the center of the stage. Let us remind ourselves
once more that Gutiérrez does not see this praxis as identical
with the overall tradition of the life of the Church, although in
some places he seems to suggest something like this.

What, then, does he tell us of the word of God? Of course,
we have seen that he never explicitly speaks of the primacy of
revealed fact. On the other hand, we have seen how he resists
the doctrinal aspect of both faith and theology. Let us look at
the texts.

> In this light the understanding of the faith appears not as
> the understanding of the simple affirmation—almost

memorization—of truths, but of a commitment, an overall
attitude, a particular posture toward life. . . .

The goal is to balance and even to reject the primacy
and almost exclusiveness which doctrine has enjoyed in
Christian life.

Note that in these texts what should not be an alternative is
made into one. By this method the doctrinal aspect is sacrificed,
but in order to hide what he is doing Gutiérrez takes care to
juxtapose a caricature of doctrinal content and the real thing.
In this way he can dispose of both the real thing and the caricature, while leaving us with the impression that he is only opposed to the excesses. He is a clever writer. At the beginning of
this study I said it is difficult to argue with him, but one thing
is clear: we will never find an outright affirmation that theology
has to study the mystery of God.

Let us turn now to the second aspect. From what standpoint
is theological judgment exercised? Is it in the light of the word
or in the light of praxis? It would help if our author defined his
viewpoint. If he were to read what he has written, he would find
more than one surprising contradiction in his work. Sometimes,
for example, he tells us that theological judgment is made in the
light of faith, at other times in the light of praxis. Finally, what
are we left with? Let us look again at the texts.

Reflection in the light of faith must constantly accompany
the pastoral action of the Church. On the other hand
theology by pointing to the sources of revelation helps to
orient pastoral activity. . . .

Theological reflection . . . would then necessarily be a
criticism . . . worked out in the light of the Word, accepted
in faith.

In these texts the light behind the judgment is the light of
faith. Faith judges commitment and this becomes theology, although these texts concede primacy to revelation and faith. We
need not go into the question of whether this view of historic

reality in the light of faith fulfills the requirements of theological
science, since in this sense anyone who observes events in the
light of faith, as every Christian in the world should do, is a
theologian. Let us concede that in this "viewpoint," if not in the
matter under consideration, these texts mention the primacy of
faith, but let us recall what we have already said on the content
of this faith. It is defined as "commitment," as "attitude toward
life." It would therefore seem that this commitment, attitude,
and praxis are what in fact judge commitment, praxis, and
attitude. Surely this is a contradiction in terms?

Let us go back to the words of Gutiérrez:

> This has led to a more biblical view of the act of faith as
> an act of trust, a going out of oneself, a commitment to
> God and neighbour, a relationship with others.

The author is beginning to pay dearly for the bad use he has
made of texts from Spicq and Alfaro, trying to tell us—through
them—something they did not say, as we have seen in examining his method of using quotations. What, then, is this faith that
sheds light? Is it action? It is said to be experience, but what is
the content of this experience? Because he has departed from the
concept of "understanding of truth" and has replaced this with
the concept of verification under the auspices of the philosophy
of action and praxis, he finds himself in a maze from which there
is no way out:

> Moreover, only by doing this truth will our faith be
> verified.

We have granted the verbal mention of the primacy of the
viewpoint of faith in the texts quoted, but now, also verbally, the
contradiction gradually emerges. This has been brought about
through the use of alternatives, where there should not be alternatives but integration:

> The goal is to balance and even to reject the primacy and
> almost exclusiveness which doctrine has enjoyed in Chris-
> tian life.

In passing, we should ask what is to be rejected, the primacy or
the exclusiveness?

Let us take another text:

> A theology which has as its points of reference only
> "truths" which have been established once and for all—
> and not the Truth which is also the way—can only be
> static and in the long run sterile.

Again, in passing, is this a genuine alternative or should the two
concepts be integrated?

These texts again show the separation that is being prepared
and the gradual distancing of the author from the concept of
revelation as a central point of reference. He appears, as we have
seen, to be separating himself from a caricature of doctrinal
content, not from the true content. But let us not be ingenuous.
He is really separating himself from doctrinal content through
his caricature of it.

If the contradiction is not very clear so far, it will become
clear in the following texts. The first prepares the way for the
second:

> Theology thus understood, that is to say as linked to
> praxis, fulfils a prophetic function insofar as it interprets
> historical events with the intention of revealing and pro-
> claiming their profound meaning.

Here it is not faith that does the judging but theology, linked to
praxis. It is not clear which is subordinate. The two are linked.

But let us observe the contradiction: until now it had been
theology, together with praxis, that performed the observation,
but now he tells us that theology should be "based on this
observation":

> But if theology is based on this observation of historical
> events and contributes to the discovery of their meaning,
> it is with the purpose of making the Christian's commit-
> ment within them more radical and clear.

Then he takes the next step:

> In the last analysis the true interpretation of the meaning
> revealed by theology is achieved only in historical praxis.
> We have here a political hermeneutics of the Gospel.

We are perhaps justified in asking what remains of what he
had previously told us about theology—in the light of *faith*,
accompanying pastoral activity, or the phrase that defined theological reflection as a critical theory in the light of the word
accepted in faith. I think the contradiction is patent. In some
texts it is faith, the word of God, and in others "praxis" that
holds the primacy of viewpoint from which judgment is to be
made.

If, after this analysis, we refer to the two methods that exist,
which we examined following the ideas of Guitton and Congar,
which of them does Gutiérrez adopt? Unless he accepts the
contradiction we have pointed out in his verbal expressions and
in his content, his method is surely that of the "heterodox
innovators" who claim to establish mechanical adaptation in
place of true renovation through a return to tradition. The
former is precisely the method that leads to schism and that did
so much harm to the Church in the second century. It is the
method proper to Gnosticism, and one that still threatens the
Church today.

Let it not be said that I am alarmist; but what good can come
from an attack on the "formal object" of faith, if one forgets that
the Mystery must be the center of hermeneutics? What must
happen if the gospel is accepted, modified, and interpreted
through .a "praxis" which even Gutiérrez cannot find the
strength or clarity to define but which, nevertheless, displays
considerable parallels with Soviet Marxism?

"We have here a political hermeneutics of the Gospel," Gutiérrez tells us. This "new approach to theology," as he also tells us explicitly, involves *redefinition* of the wisdom function and the rational knowledge function of theology, a redefinition brought about by and in the context of "historical praxis." This redefinition will apply not only to theology but also, logically, to the gospel itself:

> It is in reference to this praxis that an understanding of spiritual growth, based on scripture, should be developed. And it is through this same praxis that faith encounters the problems posed by human reason.

So we see that the riches of the whole theological tradition—in which one would think there is a more mature approach than is offered us in this "new theology"—have to be redefined. Centuries of the word of God, accepted as stemming from the mystery of the love of the Father, made flesh in genuine human reason, and yielding the fruits of a true theology—which is not to say that it is not capable of growth—are to be reread today in the light of "praxis." Personally, I do not accept the change of viewpoint offered here, which "will perhaps give us [a] solid and permanent, albeit modest, foundation."

Finally, this theory is presented as a "theology of the future." Quoting Harvey Cox, Gutiérrez tells us that "the only future that theology has, one might say, is to become the theology of the future," which Gutiérrez understands as a "critical reading of historical praxis." In what light is this "reading" to be made? The author sets it out clearly:

> To reflect on the basis of the historical praxis of liberation is to reflect in the light of the future which is believed in and hoped for. It is to reflect with a view to action which transforms the present.

And a few lines earlier he told us:

> To reflect upon a forward-directed action is not to concentrate on the past. It does not mean being the caboose of the present, rather it is to penetrate present reality, the movement of history, that which is driving history toward the future.

So the theology of eschatology is nothing other than "the theology of the future"—an eschatology and a future which do not "concentrate on the past." This, as we have seen, is to present an eschatology which breaks with that event of the past, Christ, who contains the fullness of the ages in himself, because he is God, entering into history—the eternal, the divine, the fullness becoming flesh at a particular moment which, for us, is history. This is why Gutiérrez makes no mention of the means by which contact with the past is established, such as the apostolic succession or the reenactment of the mysteries of Christ through the sacraments. Thus the sacraments, in this "new theology," would come to mean only a sanction of present events or denunciation of what is bad in "historical praxis." His theology of eschatology and the future has its roots "where the pulse of history is beating at this moment," he tells us. But where is this to be found? In "praxis," he will tell us. And how is this to be found? In the light of "praxis."

Besides the vicious circle this implies, the poverty of this "new theology" is apparent. What will be the theology of hope that underpins this "theology of the future," contained in the present? We easily suspect what it might be.

Conclusion

We share the author's "social anxiety" in response to the love of God. We, too, want to be committed, struggling to serve Christ and our brothers. We, too, see our Christianity as committing us to the struggle for integral liberation of man, including Latin American man. We know that both our Christian hope and its commitment to the common struggle of humanity to transform the world try to fulfill the requirements of human existence in the economic order as well.

I agree that the dignity of man can hardly be achieved without the resonance of the gospel message in the sphere of economic liberation. Since poverty is an assault on the dignity of man, we must, as Christians, commit ourselves, and this means committing ourselves in this world to the integral liberation of man.

What I cannot accept, however, is the change in the so-called theology that Gutiérrez offers—because what he offers is not theology. This is the conclusion to which my analysis led me. It is fine for Gustavo Gutiérrez to feel—as all of us should feel—a desire to remedy and transform the situation of injustice and poverty we live in, as in Latin America. But is it necessary to empty theology of its content in order to achieve this? There are theologians who collaborate effectively in the integral liberation of man precisely through performing a genuine theological service, by giving primacy to revealed fact and its genuine interpretation.

Before I finish I should like to point out, if only in passing, what might happen if this "new theology" is accepted in evangelization, catechesis, and Christian prayer—all of which are essential tasks in the life of an apostle.

Evangelization, which is the specific mission of the Church, is ordained to bring faith in Jesus Christ alive in the heart of men. This faith, on man's part, primarily entails a conversion of the heart. The man who comes to believe is, above all, a man who changes his heart and his whole life toward the living God, whose coming he has recognized and whose call and word he has listened to. But if faith is, above all, conversion, it is also adherence to a particular content of revelation in order to participate in and commune with the very life of God. Now in this area of communion, faith feeds on and, at the same time, needs a theology that comes from reflection on the word of God, with all the doctrinal richness this enshrines. If the doctrinal content of theology is reduced to a state of poverty, what will become of the evangelization that theology is supposed to support? We can imagine it, and its consequences will be particularly grave in Latin America in view of the religious ignorance that persists there.

Congar has made an important observation which should make us realize our responsibility in evangelization. The men who today support the praxis of sociopolitical liberation, and even Marxism, have generally been formed in the faith and within a Church that is secure in its bases. This means that their thought and behavior still have a certain equilibrium. But if we turn from the men of this generation, enriched by a solid intellectual formation, to the men of the future, we can see nothing but radicalism, that is, lack of equilibrium, since they will have received only political militancy as a way of knowledge and life.

We can also suspect the consequences which this "theology," characterized by its reticence on doctrinal matters, will have for prayer. When theology cannot enlighten man's knowledge of the living God, is it not losing one of its true objectives?

The themes of evangelization and prayer deserve much fuller attention, which are beyond the scope of this work. However, I hope I have indicated what might follow from wholesale acceptance of the "theology" of Gustavo Gutiérrez in its most basic points. My reason for undertaking this critical study has been a hope that we may thereby advance in greater fidelity to the truth of the gospel.

Notes

Notes to Introduction

1. G. Gutiérrez, *A Theology of Liberation* (New York: Orbis Books, 1973, and London: SCM Press, 1974). I concentrate on chap. 1, "Theology: A Critical Reflection," pp. 3–15.

2. Cf. G. Cottier, *Difficultés d'une théologie de la libération* (Paris, 1974), p. 81. Despite his criticism of Gutiérrez, Cottier shares his purpose: to remind the Church of its duty to fight injustice.

3. A. López Trujillo, *Teología liberadora en América Latina* (Bogotá, 1974), p. 9.

4. Cf. J. Grootaers, "La fonction théologique du laïc dans l'Eglise," in *Le Service théologique dans l'Eglise* (Paris, 1974), pp. 83–112; Y.-M. Congar, *Jalons pour une théologie du laïcat* (Paris, 1974), pp. 427–32. Congar shows both the advantages and the limits of a lay theology.

5. M. Arias Reyero, "¿Teología de la liberación o liberación de la teología?" in *Teología y Vida,* XIII (1972), 178.

6. C. Geffré, "A Prophetic Theology," editorial in *Concilium,* 6:10 (U.S. 96) (June 1974), 7–16. There is the same "closing the door" on European judgment on Latin American theology in an article by Enrique Dussel: "Today, the prophetic faith of Latin America shows it as dependent and alienated, a situation which stems from the sin of centuries. This faith knows where the idol resides and what road to liberation it must proclaim. In this task, present-day European theology can be of little or no help. Above all, the presence in Latin America of European theologians who, without knowing the reality of Latin America, or its history or temperament, presume to teach Christian 'doctrine,' can only be harmful and prejudicial. We should tell them that they are committing a basic error of methodology.

"These theologians make statements and pose problems that are relevant to Europe but not to Latin America. This is the last fruit of a pedagogical domination that we must put a stop to once and for all.

We would ask these European theologians—fraternal charity prevents me from naming them—to stop having the cheek to go to Latin America, since they will commit there (and far more culpably, centuries later) the same errors as accompanied the original conquest and which Las Casas castigated so strongly." *Histoire de la foi chrétienne et changement social en Amérique Latine* (Paris, 1975), p. 95.

7. Geffré, art. cit., p. 12.

8. Ibid., p. 11.

9. Ibid., p. 12

10. Cottier, art. cit., n. 18. Congar has shown that one of the traits that characterizes human attitudes today is to give greater importance to sincerity than to truth, to particular effectiveness than to the deeper but hidden effectiveness. He notes the risks attendant on this approach in *Vraie et fausse réforme dans l'Eglise,* pp. 382–91.

11. Y.-M. Congar, *Un peuple messianique: Salut et Libération* (Paris, 1975); also see the proposals of the permanent council of the French hierarchy in *Libérations des hommes et salut en Jésus Christ* (Paris, 1975).

Notes to Chapter 1

1. Gutiérrez, *A Theology of Liberation,* p. 3.

2. Ibid.

3. Ibid., n. 2, p. 16.

4. Ibid., p. 3.

5. Ibid.

6. Ibid., p. 4.

7. Ibid.

8. Ibid.

9. Ibid.

10. Ibid., p. 5. Gutiérrez presents these words as a quote from Congar, *Foi et théologie,* giving the reference as p. 238. But the only index reference to Abelard is much earlier, and the quote is not exact. See his n. 11, p. 16.

11. Gutiérrez, op. cit., p. 5. See n. 12, p. 16, for sources claimed.

12. Ibid. See n. 13, p. 16, for sources claimed.

13. Ibid. See n. 14, p. 16.

14. Ibid.

15. Ibid., p. 6. See n. 14, p. 16.

16. Ibid., p. 6.
17. Ibid.
18. *Gaudium et Spes,* n. 4.
19. Gutiérrez, op. cit., p. 9. See n. 32, p. 18.
20. Ibid., p. 10.
21. Ibid., p. 11.
22. Ibid., p. 12.
23. Ibid.
24. Ibid., p. 13. See n. 41, p. 19.
25. Ibid. See n. 45, p. 19.
26. Ibid., p. 14. See n. 46, p. 19.
27. Ibid., p. 15.

Notes to Chapter 2

1. See notes to Gutiérrez, *A Theology of Liberation,* pp. 15–19.

2. Yet, as has been pointed out, he does not discuss these groups and their achievements. Cf. M. Arias Reyero, "¿Teología de la liberación o liberación de la teología?" in *Teología y Vida,* XII (1972–73), 181.

3. An originality questioned by López Trujillo in his *Teología liberadora en América Latina* (Bogotá, 1974), p. 11, who claims that the most widespread form of this theology owes more to European, particularly French, sources than to indigenous sources.

4. M.-D. Chenu, O.P., *Introduction a l'étude de Saint Thomas d'Aquin* (Paris–Montreal, 1956), pp. 106–31.

5. The original Spanish edition was criticized for inaccuracies, lack of index, etc. The English edition has remedied these defects, which were partly corrected in the second Spanish edition of 1972. (Trans.)

6. Gutiérrez, op. cit., nn. to chap. 1, pp. 15–19.

7. Ibid., n. 12, p. 16. (The author's strictures on other notes do not apply to the English edition, in which the references have been expanded. Trans.)

8. Ibid., pp. 7–8; n. 25, p. 17.

9. Ibid., p. 10.

10. J.-Y. Congar, *Situation et tâches présentes de la théologie* (Paris, 1967), p. 27.

11. Gutiérrez, op. cit., p. 12; see n. 40, p. 19.

12. The reference is to Chenu, "La théologie au Saulchoir," in *La Parole de Dieu* (Paris, 1964), 1:259.

13. Gutiérrez, op. cit., p. 8.

14. Chenu, op. cit., p. 245.

15. Ibid.

16. Ibid., p. 260.

17. Gutiérrez, op. cit., p. 7.

18. See nn. 18 and 19, p. 17. Note that no volume or page reference is given to Spicq, nor to the other authorities referred to in n. 18.

19. J. Alfaro, S.J., "Fides in terminología bíblica," in *Gregorianum*, 42, 3 (1961), 504, q.v. for list of authorities cited in support of this view.

20. My italics.

21. My italics.

22. Alfaro, op. cit., pp. 504–5.

Notes to Chapter 3

1. Gutiérrez, op. cit., p. 4.

2. On the trinitarian doctrine of St Augustine, see, inter alia, my *Génesis de la doctrina sobre el Espíritu Santo . . .* (Mexico, 1966), accepted as a doctoral thesis by the University of Fribourg, 1965.

3. Y.-M. Congar, *La foi et la théologie* (Tournai, 1962). Congar adduces other studies, besides the quotes from Irenaeus, in support of his view.

4. Ibid. Congar is referring to the period between the Council of Nicaea (325) and St. Gregory the Great (604) and St. John Damascene (749).

5. See ibid. Congar shows how, in the twelfth century, a monastic and a Scholastic theology existed alongside one another. See my *Génesis . . .* (op. cit., n. 2 above).

6. H. von Baltasar, "Théologie et sainteté," in *Dieu Vivant*, 12:15–31.

7. Gutiérrez, op. cit., p. 5.

8. *ST* I, q. 1 a 6, ad 3.

9. Cf. J. H. Nicolas, *Dieu connu comme inconnu* (Paris, 1966), pp. 395–419. Nicolas speaks with great precision of "notional theology" and "mystical theology," by which he does not mean the knowledge that theology provides of the heights of spiritual experience but knowledge of God in his mystery, not in function of the laws of notional

theology but by way of supernatural contemplation, based on affective union with God, "*quasi* experimental knowledge."

10. *ST* I, q. 1 a 6, ad 3; II–II, q. IV a 8, ad 3; q VIII a 5, ad 3.

11. P. 5.

12. P. 6. See his notes, pp. 14–17.

13. M. F. Navares, "El concepto de teología en S. Tomás," in *Rev. Théol. Limense* (May–Aug. 1974), pp. 119–25. On this point, see also R. Gagnebet, "La nature de la théologie spéculative," in *Rev. Théol.*, 44 (1938), 1–39, 213–55, 645–74; M. Labourdette, "La théologie intelligence de la foi," in *Rev. Théol.*, 46 (1946), 5–44; Y.-M. Congar, "Théologie," in *DTC*, 447–83; J. H. Nicolas, op. cit. For St. Thomas' actual thought, see *De Trinitate de Boecio*, proem., q II, a 2; q V, a 4; one should also bear the treatise on faith in mind: I–II, q 2, a 10.

14. Nicolas, op. cit., p. 264.

15. Ibid., p. 266; St. Thomas, II–II, q 2, a 10.

16. Nicolas, op. cit., quotes a very clear text from St. Thomas on p. 306, where he comments: " 'Discourse' implies 'multiplicity' and 'order.' "

17. Cf. M. Labourdette, art. cit., pp. 37–38.

18. Cf. Congar, art. cit.; Chenu, "La théologie au Saulchoir."

19. Ibid. Why, as Gutiérrez quotes Chenu, has he not taken this aspect into account? The same applies to the use he makes of Congar's article "Théologie."

20. Cf. Congar, art. cit., pp. 450–51; Navares, art. cit., pp. 122–25; cf. *ST* I, q I, a 3 and 7.

21. On this point I am summarizing the arguments of Nicolas, op. cit., pp. 273–75. His establishment of a close link between theology and the beatific vision throws light on both the object of theology and its contemplative nature.

22. Nicolas, op. cit., p. 307, n. 46, quotes Cayetano, Bañez, and Labourdette to show that the idea of subalternation implies two things: on one hand, the imperfect state of theology; on the other, its dynamic thrust toward the greater clarity that will be obtained in the beatific vision.

23. These statements are taken from Chenu, *Is Theology a Science?* (London and New York, 1959), which Gutiérrez also quotes, but with what understanding of this aspect?

24. Op. cit., p. 6.

25. Chenu, op. cit., p. 69.

26. Cf., inter alia, Congar, art. cit.; H. Chavannes, *L'analogie entre Dieu et le monde selon St Thomas d'Aquin et selon K. Barth* (Paris, 1969), pp. 228–38; Nicolas, *Dieu connu comme inconnu,* pp. 237–316.

27. A. Feuillet, *Le mystère de l'amour divin dans la théologie Johannique,* (Paris, 1972), p. 60, quoting L. Malevez, "La théologie fonctionelle et NT," in *RSR,* 48 (1960), 287–88.

28. Inter alia, C. Geffré, "Declin et renouveau de la théologie dogmatique," in *Le point théologique* (Paris, 1971), pp. 21–43. He has been criticized for his approach by M. Corvez in "Théologie fondamentale," in *Rev. Théol.,* 73 (1973), 453–55; M.-J. Le Guillou, *Le mystère du Père* (Paris, 1973), pp. 23–24; A. Patfoort, "Nouvel âge de la théologie ou . . . de l'apologétique," in *Angelicum,* 50 (1973), 243–48.

29. These arguments are taken from Nicolas, "La théologie," in *L'universite et l'integration du savoir* (Fribourg, 1972), pp. 46–48. Nicolas shares Maritain's views on the relationship between philosophy and theology. Both, naturally, go back to the same source, viz., St. Thomas Aquinas. Cf. J. Maritain, *An Introduction to Philosophy* (London, 1930), pp. 124–32.

30. Cf. Congar, *La foi et la théologie,* pp. 235–38; M. Corvez, "Philosophie et théologie," in *Rev. Théol.,* 73 (1973), 595–608.

31. Cf. Maritain, op. cit., pp. 136–37.

32. Corvez, art. cit., p. 599.

33. Cf. Decree on Priestly Formation, 15. Also Paul VI, Inaugural Address to the Second General Conference of the Latin American Episcopate.

34. Cf. Maritain, "Science et philosophie," in *Quatre Essais sur l'esprit dans sa condition charnelle* (Paris, 1956), pp. 169–256.

35. Cf. D. Dubarle, *Bases para una teología de la ciencia* (Barcelona, 1969), pp. 65–67. He is not dealing specifically with sociology, but this is still confined within the narrow limits of what can be observed, unless one is dealing with social philosophy. But Gutiérrez opposes sociology to philosophy. Even if we concede that it is a particular philosophy, it must still depend on speculative philosophy.

Notes to Chapter 4

1. Cottier, *Difficultés d'une Théologie de la Libération,* pp. 68–69. Analysis of the different meanings that can be attached to the word "liberation" fails to produce a clear concept. Rather, "the impression

given by some texts is one of a drastic reduction of the concept of ecclesial praxis to the political sphere, without much differentiation being made of this, which usually comes to mean revolutionary political praxis, aimed at victory for the Socialist system, through the inevitable instrument of Marxist methodology." Cf. A. López Trujillo, *Teología de la Liberación en América Latina* (Bogotá, 1974), pp. 66–70. See also H. Borrat, "Entre las proclamas y los programas," in *Víspera* (Montevideo, 1973), p. 50.

2. Gutiérrez, op. cit., pp. 6–7.

3. This is what Gutiérrez says and adopts as a theme (op. cit., pp. 196ff.). Congar deals with this current and some of its representatives in *Situations et Tâches,* pp. 76–87. See also Paul VI, Opening Address to the Second General Conference of Latin American Bishops; G. M. Garrone, "Les exercices spirituels dans les grands seminaires," in *Seminarium,* 2 (1968), 178.

4. Here and in the following paragraphs I am following J. H. Nicolas, *La Grâce et la Gloire* (Paris, 1971), pp. 39–40.

5. Cf. II–II, q 32, a 3.

6. Cf. A. Feuillet, *Le mystère de l'amour divin,* op. cit., pp. 89–112.

7. Cf. Nicolas, *Dieu connu comme inconnu,* pp. 377-78.

8. J. Alfaro, *Fides in Terminologica Biblica,* op. cit., pp. 504–5; C. Spicq, *Théologie morale du N.T.,* pp. 256–76, 462–70.

9. F. Braun, *Jean le théologien,* III/2, *Sa théologie. Le Christ, notre Seigneur* (Paris, 1977), pp. 121–38.

10. I. de la Potterie, "Nacer del agua y nacer del Espíritu. El texto bautismal de Jn 3.5," in *La vida según el Espíritu* (Salamanca, 1967), pp. 51–52.

11. Braun, op. cit., p. 124; M.-J. Le Guillou, *Le mystère du Père,* pp. 83–101; R. Latourelle, *Théologie de la Révélation* (Paris, 1963), pp. 383–402; L. Dewailly, *Jésus Christ parole de Dieu* (Paris, 1969), pp. 28–45; L. Charlier, "Le Christ parole de Dieu," in *La Parole de Dieu en Jésus Christ* (Tournai, 1964), pp. 121–45.

12. II–II, q 1–4.

13. Gutiérrez, op. cit., p. 11.

14. Ibid., p. 15.

15. The works to which Gutiérrez alludes, but does not mention, consist of a thesis still not published in its entirety—as Labourdette notes, in *Rev. Théol.,* 70 (1970), 443—titled "La doctrine du mépris du monde en Occident"; two volumes dealing with the eleventh century

and some complementary articles have appeared.

16. "Le mépris du monde . . . Problemes de vie religieuse," in *Rev. d'Ascétique et Morale*, vol. 22 (1965).

17. J. Daniélou, "Mépris du monde et valeurs terrestres d'après le Concile Vatican II," in op. cit., pp. 186–96.

18. Cf. J. Guy, "La place du mépris du monde dans le monachisme ancien," in ibid., pp. 5–17.

19. Ibid., p. 5.

20. K. Rahner, "Théologie et anthropologie," in *Théologie d'aujourdui et de demain* (Paris, 1967), pp. 99–120.

21. For a precise description of the disasters of subjectivity, when this becomes a general statute of thought, see Le Guillou, *Le mystère du Père*, pp. 152–65.

22. Gutiérrez, op. cit., p. 8. See our earlier comments on his use of sources.

23. Ibid. The same comments apply.

24. On the importance of the structure of the Church and the place the apostolic succession holds in it, see Le Guillou, op. cit., pp. 35–46; L. Bouyer, *L'Eglise de Dieu* (Paris, 1970), pp. 401–48. The concept is obviously not limited to its juridical legitimacy aspect, which depends "on a certain content, in which conformity to the faith of the Apostles holds the prime place. Apostolicity of mission requires apostolicity of doctrine." Cf. Congar, *Ministère et communion écclesiale* (Paris, 1971), p. 82.

25. M.-D. Chenu, "Los signos de la época," in *La Iglesia en el mundo actual* (Bilbao, 1968), pp. 95–97.

26. Chenu, op. cit.; Congar, "L'influence de la société et de l'histoire sur le dévellopement de l'homme chrétien," in *N.R.T.* (July–Aug. 1964), pp. 673–92.

27. Chenu, op. cit., pp. 107–8; G. Cottier, *La mort des idéologies et de l'ésperance* (Paris, 1970), pp. 143–49; B. Montagnes, "La parole de Dieu dans la création," in *Rev. Théol.*, 54 (1954), 213–41; idem, "Parole de Dieu et parole humaine," in *Rev. Théol.*, 52 (1952), 209–15. These two articles by Montagnes do not deal directly with "the signs of the times" but provide a firm theological basis for understanding them.

28. Chenu, op. cit., pp. 108–9.

29. *Gaudlum et Spes*, n. 4: "If, despite everything, there has to be a history of salvation, this will tend, evidently, to be understood through

an *interpretation* of profane history through the same *Word of God.*"
30. The others being M. McGrath and E. Pironio. As McGrath notes, in *La Iglesia en la transformación de América Latina a la luz del Concilio* (Bogotá, 1969), pp. 73–100, Chenu's definition of "the signs of the times," as formulated in *N.R.T.* as early as January 1965, served to clarify the meaning given to the phrase in *Gaudium et Spes.*

31. From the scriptural angle, there is a very helpful study by Feuillet on the meaning of "serving the times" and *kairós:* A. Feuillet, "Les fondements de la morale chrétienne d'après l'épître aux Romains," in *Rev. Théol.,* 70 (1970), 357–86.

32. H. Duméry, *Blondel et la religion: Essai critique sur la "Lettre" de 1886* (Paris, 1954), p. 27; idem, *Raison et religion dans la philosophie de l'action* (Paris, 1963).

33. Duméry interprets Blondel in the sense that Gutiérrez accepts, and which is the opposite from Blondel's true thought, as presented in H. Bouillard, *Blondel et le Christianisme* (Paris, 1961), and in C. Tresmontant, *Introduction a la métaphysique de Maurice Blondel* (Paris, 1963). J. H. Nicolas has reviewed these studies in different numbers of *Rev. Théol.* and I am following his thought. Without being a Blondelian, Nicolas is a theologian and philosopher who is interested in Blondelian studies.

34. J. Nicolas, reviewing Duméry's *Raison et religion . . . ,* in *Rev. Théol.,* 65 (1965), 607–9.

35. Nicolas, "Le centenaire de Maurice Blondel," in *Rev. Théol.,* 62 (1962), 438. Cf. also ibid., 54 (1954), 684; M. Blondel, *Procès de l'intélligence* (Paris, 1922), pp. 228–42.

36. For Blondel, "notional knowledge" cannot succeed in reaching being; only "real knowledge" captures the being to which intelligence aspires. Cf. op. cit., pp. 236–37.

37. By, inter alia, A. López Trujillo, G. Cottier, M. Arias Reyero, C. Bravo, and A. Martínez.

38. Quoted by H. de Lubac in *Théologie d'aujourdui et de demain,* pp. 12–13.

39. G. Widmer, quoted in de Lubac, loc. cit., p. 15.

40. De Lubac, loc. cit., p. 18.

41. Significant names in this connection are, inter alia, J. Ratzinger, A. Darlap, J. Tillard, M.-J. Le Guillou, J. Moltmann, L. Boros, H. von Baltasar, O. Cullmann, and M. Seckler.

42. J.-P. Sartre, *L'éxistentialisme est un humanisme* (Paris, 1946),

pp. 21–22, and *Les Mouches,* p. 135; cf. the fine comparative study by L. B. Geiger, "Existentialisme de Sartre et salut chrétien," in *Philosophie et Spiritualité,* II (Paris, 1963), 9–33.

43. Quoted in G. Wetter, *Le matérialisme dialectique* (Paris, 1962), p. 541.

44. The quote is from Althusser, and it is Gutiérrez who claims its views are applicable to Latin America today.

45. There are works dealing with the matter from the aspect of hope and that of salvation history. Among the authors mentioned in n. 41 above, cf. especially O. Cullmann, *Christ et le temps* (Neuchâtel, 1959), and *Le salut dans l'histoire* (Neuchâtel, 1966); M. Seckler, *Le salut et l'histoire* (Paris, 1967).

46. E. Schillebeeckx, *Christ the Sacrament of the Encounter with God* (London and New York, 1968).

47. Cf. J. Comblin, *Théologie de la pratique revolutionnaire* (Paris, 1974), p. 40: "Even the Protestants now recognize that it is impossible to draw a Christian morality from the Bible alone. One of the most pertinent criticisms that have been made of the Theologies of Revolution and of Liberation is that they ignore historical mediations and fall straight back on the Bible, notably misusing the themes of the Exodus, Prophecy, Poverty of the community, etc."

48. Quoted in Wetter, *Le matérialisme dialectique,* op. cit., p. 547.

49. Y.-M. Congar, "Salvación y liberación," in *Teología de la liberación. Conversaciones en Toledo* (Burgos, 1973), p. 196.

Notes to Chapter 5

1. Inter alia, G. Wetter, op. cit.; P. Dognin, *Initiation à Karl Marx* (Paris, n.d.); Y. Calvez, *Le Pensée de Karl Marx* (Paris, 1956); G. Cottier, *L'athéisme du jeune Marx, ses origines hégeliennes* (Paris, 1959); A. López Trujillo, *La concepción del hombre en Marx* (Bogotá, 1972). J. Comblin, op. cit., p. 33, says: "Marxism has sometimes been compared to Aristotelianism. The integration of Marxist rationalism in a possible conception . . . would be the equivalent of the interpretation of Aristotelianism in medieval scholasticism. Now, the comparison goes further than those who normally make it imagine. St. Thomas, when he took on the philosophy of Aristotle, left none of its concepts intact, but profoundly changed them all, as being non-apt to the evangelical message he was trying to express. If the comparison is to hold,

all Marxist concepts would have to be changed likewise." Although his remarks on St. Thomas' use of Aristotle may need some modifying, it is true that St. Thomas took a critical and selective view of Aristotle; this criticism and selection are what is missing from Gutiérrez's analysis of Marxism.

2. Pope John XXIII, *Mater et Magistra,* n. 18: "Both the employees and directors of an enterprise should base their relationships on the principles of human solidarity and Christian brotherhood, since both competition in the economic liberal sense of the word and the class struggle in the Marxist sense are contrary to nature and opposed to a Christian concept of life."

3. J. Guitton, *La pensée moderne et le catholicisme,* III, "La pensée de M. Loisy" (Aix, 1936), pp. 57–59.